FOREWORD BY PATRICK EWING

EVERYBODY NEEDS A
HEAD
"COACH"

"Go Beacon"

Coach Mike Jarvis

"Let Your Light Shine"

COACH MIKE JARVIS
with Chad Bonham

EVERYBODY NEEDS A HEAD COACH

Copyright © 2015 Cross Training Publishing

ISBN 978-1-938254-40-6

EVERYBODY NEEDS A HEAD COACH / Chad Bonham
Published by Cross Training Publishing,
Omaha, Nebraska 68137

Distributed in the United States and Canada by Cross Training
Publishing

This book is manufactured in the United States of America.

CONTENTS

DEDICATION

I would like to dedicate this book to Connie, my wife and best friend. Your love, support, and encouragement have made it possible for me to pursue my dreams and live a blessed life. – *Coach Mike Jarvis*

ACKNOWLEDGEMENTS

First of all, I would like to thank God for allowing me to be born, raised, and educated in the United States of America.

Thanks to my mother, Dorothy, who taught me how to love, pray, and laugh.

To my big brother Richard, my sister Trudy, and my little brother Stephen, I would like to thank you for your friendship and support.

To Connie, thanks for being a great wife, mother, grandmother and friend.

Thanks to all of the men and women who have taught, coached, or ministered to me.

Thanks to all the men and women who have assisted me with my teams and all of the young men who have allowed me to coach them.

A special thanks to Joel Feldman, Kathy Datelle, and everyone that has taken the time to read, critique, and edit the sample chapters. Thanks again and again!

Last but not least, I would like to thank Chad Bonham for helping me write a book that will glorify our Lord and Savior, Jesus Christ. – *Coach Mike Jarvis*

I would like to thank Mike Jarvis for giving me the chance to help tell his incredible story. Working with Coach Jarvis has been a privilege and an honor, and I look forward to partnering with him on more exciting projects in the future.

I am also grateful for the undying support of my wife, Amy, who pushed me to stay on task and took care of many household responsibilities that allowed me the extra time to work on this book. She and my sons Lance, Cole and Quinn are my daily inspiration!

As always, I want to acknowledge the incredible influence of my mom and dad, Stan and Betty Bonham. Although they are no longer here to see the full return on their investment, they will always be responsible for anything good that ever comes out of my life.

Additional thanks go to Gordon Thiessen at Cross Training Publishing for catching the vision for this book and lending his expertise and enthusiasm to the project.

And finally, I want to make sure to give God the praise for blessing me with these undeserved gifts and talents and providing the platform from which I have hopefully been able to bring glory to His name. – *Chad Bonham*

FOREWORD
By Patrick Ewing

When I was 12 years old, my mother moved from Kingston, Jamaica, to Boston so she could make a better life for our family. At that time, foreigners could apply for a temporary work visa and then, when their time was up, they could get sponsored and extend their stay within the United States. After working as a nanny, my mother took advantage of the opportunity and took a new job at Massachusetts General Hospital. She saved her money and sent for my father and my older sister. As she was financially able, the rest of us came one or two at a time until our entire family was finally together again.

It was 1975 when I made the trip to Boston. I briefly attended Webster Grammar School before moving to the Cambridge Achievement School in seventh grade. That's where Steve Jenkins, my seventh and eighth-grade basketball coach, first introduced me to Coach Jarvis. It was the start of a very meaningful relationship in my life.

For the next three years, Coach Jarvis met with me privately to help me better learn the game and develop my skills as a post player. He taught me about Bill Russell and other great NBA centers and told me that I too could one day become an elite athlete.

Coach Jarvis took over the basketball program at Cambridge Rindge and Latin at the beginning of my sophomore year. It was during those three years that I truly was able to recognize his work ethic and his deep knowledge of the game. Coach Jarvis was a great teacher. Our entire team looked up to him and listened to the things he said, and then we tried our best to successfully do those things on the court.

One thing I especially enjoyed was the family atmosphere we had on our team. A lot of that came from his wife Connie and their kids, Mike and Dana. We often went over to their house to eat meals and watch movies together. They were great people and always made us feel at home.

During that second season in 1979, the Massachusetts Interscholastic Athletic Association tried to keep our team out of the state championship tournament. Coach Jarvis had been accused of illegally recruiting Karl Hobbs, one of our star players, to play for our team. Coaching in itself is a very stressful job no matter what level. Yet somehow, Coach Jarvis was able to shield the players from the controversial legal issues that were surrounding our program. We never really talked about it as a team. Instead, Coach Jarvis kept us focused on our books and basketball as we prepared for the state tournament.

During my senior season, when I was starting to think about college ball, Coach Jarvis was instrumental in helping me make some important decisions. My mother had a great deal of respect for him. She took his advice and so did I. My career took off at Georgetown and it became apparent I would have a career in the NBA. A lot of coaches might have tried to take advantage of that situation, but Coach Jarvis never asked me for anything then and he has never asked anything of me since.

Coach Jarvis was an integral part of my early development as a player. Along with all the other coaches I've had in my life, he helped me lay a foundation and become the person that I am today. As you read this book, I hope Coach Jarvis' experiences inspire you to find your purpose in life. I also hope his story challenges you to find someone you can mentor and influence just like he did for me in my life.

INTRODUCTION
Everybody Has A Story

Everybody needs something. We all have basic physical needs like food, clothing, shelter, sunlight and air. Beyond that, no matter how independent we might like to think we are at times, we also have emotional needs, educational needs, relational needs and, yes, spiritual needs.

It took me a while to fully grasp the need for the last item on that list–60 years to be exact. My spiritual rebirth happened during the time I was experiencing my first major absence away from basketball as a head coach. It was also during that time that I first became interested in telling my story.

In particular, my wife Connie encouraged me to reminisce about my time at Cambridge Rindge and Latin High School where I coached Patrick Ewing and his teammates to three consecutive Massachusetts state titles. Connie went to the garage and pulled out a scrapbook that she had put together with all the newspaper articles from those years in Cambridge. In front of me were all of the facts and information from those glory days.

It also brought back memories of the difficulty that our program faced during my second season when false accusations of illegally recruiting a player from another school almost cost our team a chance at the state championship, not to mention almost cost me my career.

That led to an interesting conversation with Richard Rappaport, an entertainment attorney I had recently met in Boca Raton. He encouraged me to write a screenplay about that season. My wife thought it was a wonderful idea. After all, I knew the ending of the story, and it was a good ending. It was easy for me to go back and relive it.

Over the course of two years, Richard and I met in his office and went over the articles. The result was a screenplay called *Court of*

Kings. It was about one incredibly important year. It was a trying time and yet it was a triumphant time. I didn't realize how much had taken place until I started putting it into words.

After spending some time working at ESPN as a studio analyst, I found my way back to the bench thanks to a unique opportunity in my new hometown. In 2008, I took over as the head coach at Florida Atlantic University. Two years later, a writer who was working for Fellowship of Christian Athletes reached out to me about contributing to a book called *Greatest Coach Ever*. Chad Bonham was serving as the primary editor and ghost writer for the project and had been told I might have some insight into the book's subject matter: legendary UCLA basketball coach John Wooden.

The book was released in 2011 and that same year, Chad approached me about a follow-up project called *Greatest Leader Ever*. In that book, I was one of 40 people to share a key leadership principle based on the life of Christ. As Chad and I stayed in touch, we began discussing my screenplay and my desire to write a book that would share some of my stories and how they relate to key biblical principles.

In 2014, it became apparent that my time at FAU was coming to a close, so I decided to move forward and start putting things into motion. It wasn't the timing that I had planned, but it has turned out to be in God's perfect timing as I have entered into the next stage of my life.

As you read this book, there are a few important things I hope you learn:

1. Everybody has a story. That means *everybody*. You don't have to be a former basketball coach, a famous athlete, a celebrated entertainer, an award-winning musician, a decorated soldier, an accomplished politician, or a revered spiritual leader to have something interesting to share about your life. You are here for a purpose, and part of that purpose is to live out the story that God has planned for your life.

2. Everybody's story is God's story: Your story should point people back to what He has done in your life. Testimonies, conversations and narratives conveyed through the written word have power. They can't be refuted. For those of us who are Christians, we know the ending of our story, and it's a good ending.

3. Everybody needs to tell his or her story: Whenever possible, we should try to put our stories in black and white. There are so many important things that happen in our lives. If we don't write them down, we may not remember them. As we get older, we lose some of those memories. Eventually, there's going to come a day and time when we won't be around anymore. Don't let your history and your legacy get lost. Share your story. Whether through written or oral dissertation, pass it down to the next generation.

What you are about to read is my story. It follows my journey as a son, a brother, an athlete, a husband, a father, a basketball coach and, most importantly, a follower of Christ. This book represents the mostly hard lessons I have learned along the way.

Each chapter takes a look at a different biblical principle I have gleaned while looking back at the many things God has brought me through. These principles represent basic needs we all have such as humility, commitment, determination, encouragement, respect, purpose, community, and grace. At the end of each chapter, there are some questions you can go over on your own or in a small group setting. I pray that this time of reflection will be beneficial to your soul.

The most important thing I hope to accomplish through this book, however, is to point you to the source of all your needs. I finally understood and embraced that truth back in 2005 when I was born again.

Everybody Needs A Head Coach!
And His name is Jesus Christ.

CHAPTER ONE

THE BEST WORST DAY OF MY LIFE
Everybody Needs Humility

"It was pride that changed angels into devils; it is humility that makes men as angels." – Saint Augustine

On June 22, 2014, I stood before a packed house at The Journey Church in Boca Raton, Florida. It was Father's Day, but my message wasn't exclusively for dads. My message was for anyone who wanted to hear *my* journey and anyone who needed to hear the Gospel. As I began speaking, I reminded everyone there that I wasn't a preacher. I was a basketball coach who loved to tell stories, and I simply wanted to share my life experiences.

A few days later, the pastor informed me that six people accepted Christ. It was a blessing to know God was able to use my story to help others make such an important decision.

If you'd asked me 10 years earlier whether this was even possible, I would have shaken my head in disbelief. Back then, I was still reeling from a sudden and unexpected departure from my job as the head men's basketball coach at St. John's University and false allegations of impropriety that the New York media was reporting.

So before I can go any deeper into my story and the incredible journey that God has led me through, I need to talk about the big question that those within the college basketball community still ask to this day: What happened at St. John's?

The answer to that question isn't about vindication or setting the record straight, although that is important to me. It's really about sharing a bigger message regarding the devastating impact that pride had on my life and how I am still learning to embrace the Christ-centered principle of humility.

The King of New York

In 1978, I was named head boy's basketball coach at my alma mater Rindge Technical High School (later changed to Cambridge Rindge and Latin) in Cambridge, Massachusetts. It was the fulfillment of a decade's long dream. Thanks to some great players like Patrick Ewing, Karl Hobbs, and Rumeal Robinson, that job set me on an upward trajectory which included stops at Boston University, The George Washington University and finally, in 1998, St. John's University.

I had gone from an aspiring young coach who couldn't get an interview for any coaching job to taking one of the premier head coaching positions in America. The day after my press conference, the *New York Daily News* ran a picture of me with a crown superimposed onto my head. The editors proclaimed me as "The King of New York!"

In the fall of 2003, I was about to start my fifth season at St. John's. We had made three NCAA appearances, including the Elite Eight in 1999 and had just won the National Invitational Tournament (NIT) a few months earlier. I had several television interviews lined up to promote my first book *Skills For Life*, co-written with Jonathan Peck. A film in which I had a cameo, *The Perfect Score*, was soon to hit theaters.

I was also in the middle of contract negotiations for a multi-million, multi-year contract extension, and there were a number of endorsement deals in the works. I had become so visible in New York that it was kind of scary. From my perspective, I was on top of the college basketball world.

It's hard to say when my attitude shifted, but somewhere along the way, I started to believe the hype. I started to believe that I could accomplish anything. Winning a national championship and being recognized as a great coach became more important to me than the reasons why I first started coaching. Noble ideals such as doing it for the love of the game and preparing my players for life after basketball became secondary to my personal goals.

Being in New York only exacerbated the problem. I got caught up in the glitz and glamour of the Big Apple. I got caught up in the money and the attention I was receiving. I had become attracted to the bright lights.

In Proverbs 16:18, King Solomon wrote these poignant words: "Pride comes before destruction, and an arrogant spirit before a fall" (HCSB). As I reached the pinnacle of success, I became guilty of having too much pride and getting too much satisfaction in what I was accomplishing. That was part of a hard lesson I was about to learn.

Collapse of a Kingdom

On December 8, 2001, we headed to Madison Square Garden for a game against Manhattan College. The cross-town matchup was one of the school's longest standing rivalries but was historically lopsided in St. John's favor. Although both teams came into the contest with just one loss each, we remained the heavy favorites to win.

Someone forgot to tell Manhattan.

The Jaspers played inspired basketball and defeated us handily, 85-68. Manhattan went on a 12-game winning streak and received an invitation to the NIT. When I had a chance to speak to head coach Bobby Gonzalez after the game, I made a humorous but self-prophesying remark.

"Bobby, be careful," I said. "You are now the 'King of New York!' And you know what happens to kings. They get their heads cut off."

It's so true. As soon as a king takes over the throne, he and his kingdom are instantly vulnerable to being overthrown. We've seen it throughout the ages in places like Babylon, Greece and Rome. And it always starts with pride.

At St. John's, there was plenty of blame to go around for what took place during the early stages of the 2003-04 season. We got off to a rough start on the court, winning only one of our first five games. If that wasn't bad enough, there was trouble off the court. I had to dismiss one of my starters for failing his second drug test and suspend another starter for fighting with a co-ed. "Fire Jarvis" chants surfaced amongst the fan base, and my wife became more and more depressed with each game.

Then, I made a huge mistake and allowed my pride to convince me to do an interview with host Mike Francesa on WFAN-AM radio. During the interview, I spoke about what our team had accomplished. I compared our success to the achievements of former St. John's head coach and Hall of Fame inductee Lou Carnesecca. The interview did exactly the opposite of what I intended and angered many of Lou's fans, especially university president Father Donald Harrington. He took my remarks personally and perceived them as a lack of support on my part for the men's basketball program.

However, at the crux of the conflict were two very strong-willed individuals: my agent Rob Ades and (now former) president Harrington. One happened to represent me. The other represented the university. To say that they disliked each other would be putting it mildly. It went much, much deeper than that.

During the two years prior, tensions between both parties had continued to escalate as we worked to renegotiate my original seven-year contract. Father Harrington was still upset about the initial contract negotiations and was even more upset about the fact that Rob had met with Michael Jordan to talk about the Washington Wizards' head coaching position on my behalf.

In a matter of days and weeks, everything came crashing down. It was December of 2003 when Rob went to meet with St. John's athletic director David Wegrzyn. The negotiations went so badly that St. John's decided to initiate an agreement to separate. Most were led to believe that we were parting ways because of the poor start. Later on, more accusations emerged that would even further muddy the waters of public opinion.

After my departure from St. John's, the *New York Daily News* printed an illustration that depicted Santa Claus booting me out of New York. Figuratively speaking, I had been dethroned and exiled from the city.

Because of pride, I wasn't even concerned about losing my job. I wholeheartedly believed I would get another shot to coach at a high level within a matter of months. That didn't happen. The walls had collapsed around me, and I wasn't even aware of just how bad things really were.

A Kingdom In Ruins

On February 6, 2004, my son Mike and I were in Manhattan hosting a morning ESPN2 show called *Cold Pizza*. While in the studio, we received word that, during a road trip to Pittsburgh, six of my former players snuck out of the hotel after curfew and went to a strip club. According to the report, they brought a woman back to the hotel. She then claimed that she had been raped.

It was later discovered that the alleged victim was attempting to extort the players. Her plan fell apart when one of the players used his cell phone to videotape her extortion attempt. In the meantime, my name was being linked back to the team's behavior. Some used it as a means to justify my firing six weeks earlier.

On February 8, 2004, Father Harrington spoke to Rafael Hermoso of the *New York Times*. During the interview, Harrington absolved my former assistant, who was acting as the interim head coach, of responsibility for the actions of the players. When told that his remarks seemed to be placing the blame on me, Father Harrington said, "These young men made decisions and they're responsible for those decisions. I know that Mike Jarvis would never want this to happen and I'm sure Mike would've tried to avoid it."

Unfortunately, that paled in comparison to what was on the horizon. One of the six players, Abe Keita, returned to campus to learn that he had been removed from the basketball team and suspended for a year. Since Keita wasn't a U.S. citizen and didn't have a scholarship, he was subject to deportation. Keita obtained legal representation and held a press conference where he asserted that race played a role in his punishment and that he intended to file a civil rights action against St. John's. He also claimed that he received nearly $300 a month in cash payments from a member of the basketball staff.

As a result of Keita's accusations of an extra benefit, the NCAA commenced to investigate his claims. In its own investigation, St. John's reported that not a single person, not even a teammate, came forward and reported that Keita had told them about the funds he received or that they even suspected he had received any payments.

Even before the NCAA had completed the investigation on November 26, 2004, St. John's decided to take matters into its own hands. Father Harrington announced that the university was going to self-impose a series of penalties. The men's basketball program was placed on two years of probation and was not allowed to participate in postseason competition during the 2004-05 season. Harrington also determined that St. John's would reduce the program's number of scholarships from 13 to 12 for the next two seasons. The school also forfeited 46 games in which Keita participated, due to the fact that he was deemed an ineligible student-athlete.

The NCAA probe lasted well over a year. The process cost me thousands of dollars, countless hours, and a lot of stress. It should also be noted that throughout the process Keita never showed up to testify.

On May 10, 2005, I received a letter from the NCAA, which reads as follows:

"Attached is a copy of the NCAA Division I Committee on Infractions findings of violations in which you are named, as set forth in Infractions Report No. 246 concerning St. John's University – Case No. M220. The committee did not impose a penalty on you."

I was now totally free to return to the coaching ranks if I so desired. Although several schools may have wanted to hire me, I was untouchable while the investigation was going on. By the time everything was finally over, I had become damaged goods. My reputation had been soiled, and the truth was nothing more than an afterthought.

One important piece of information that was overlooked was the fact that St. John's continued to pay me as part of our agreement to part ways. If I had been found guilty of any of the allegations, the school could have fired me with cause and would have no longer been required to pay me the remaining year and a half left on my contract.

Because of the pride exhibited by several people, myself included, my career was in shambles. The kingdom I had supposedly built was in ruins. Throughout my life, I had tried to make a difference. I had tried to teach young people about how to prepare for life after basketball, how to use basketball as a means of getting an education, and how to become something more than a basketball player. That was the case at St. John's, but at the same time I had also let my pride get the best of me and to learn firsthand that, as King Solomon teaches us in Proverbs 16:18, pride does indeed go before the fall.

When the reality set in that my name was no longer on the marquee, I started to question myself. Why was this happening to me? Why was my world crashing down? What could I have done differently or better? Where do I go from here?

I could have been pushed even deeper into pride, but instead, the situation crushed my spirit and started to break me of the selfish behavior to which I had fallen prey. God used this experience to bring me to my knees. He humbled me and opened the door for restoration and healing.

The King of Kings

The Bible shows us many examples of what happens when someone is overcome with pride. In every instance, pride led to negative circumstances that, in some cases, resulted in mortal demise. However, many of our greatest heroes of the faith overcame pride to accomplish amazing things in God's name.

Jonah, for instance, was too prideful to preach repentance to the city of Ninevah, but an encounter with a giant fish helped him see the error of his ways (Jonah 1-2).

Paul is another great example of prideful behavior that led to a life-changing encounter with God. Known at the time as Saul, the religious zealot was blinded by a heavenly light and confronted about his persecution of the growing Body of Christ. He turned from his misguided, destructive behavior and became one of history's most influential Christian leaders (Acts 9).

Ironically, it was Jesus Christ who had the right to be prideful yet was the one who showed the most humility. When Jesus came to Earth, He didn't ascend from Heaven on a white horse to violently reclaim His position as King of Kings (Revelation 19:16). Instead, Jesus came in the humblest way possible, born to a virgin girl in the most undesirable circumstances with very little fanfare (Luke 2).

Despite being God in the form of man, Jesus lived a quiet, unassuming life in Nazareth until He was ready to launch His ministry as a young man in his early 30s. Surrounding Him were men with big egos and powerful kingdoms to protect. On one hand, there were the religious leaders of the Jewish people. They rejected any new revelations and did their best to exercise the letter of the law. On the other hand, there was the Roman Empire and King Herod, who was always wary of an uprising amongst the Jews.

At first, the Romans had no concern about this so-called prophet who was preaching about God's love and redemption. The religious leaders, however, took immediate note of Jesus' following as it began to grow. They set into a motion a plan to get rid of His disruptive presence. This meant trumping up false accusations and using the Romans' fear of any disturbances amongst the Jewish population.

God knew how both sides would respond to Jesus' message. He knew that their pride would blind them from the Truth. And even as the Jews and the Romans predictably succumbed to their human nature, God was working it all out for the good of mankind. He took an act of injustice against His own Son and turned it into the plan of salvation to which we all have access today.

Jesus didn't have to come to Earth. He didn't have to offer His body to be broken. He didn't have to shed His precious blood for anyone, much less the entire human population. But because Jesus was devoid of pride, He was able to willingly lay down His life so that we could be reconciled back to God the Father.

"Though he was God, he did not think of equality with God as something to cling to. Instead, he gave up his divine privileges and took the humble position of a slave and was born as a human being. When he appeared in human form, he humbled himself in obedience to God and died a criminal's death on a cross." (Philippians 2:6-8/NLT)

Everybody Needs Humility

December 20, 2003, was the worst day of my life. That was the day I was removed as head coach at St. John's University. In reality, however, it was the best day of my life because leaving New York for Florida resulted in an encounter with Pastor David Nicholas that led to me being born again and changed forever.

What I thought was the ending was really just the beginning. Unfortunately, it took a hard fall and some time away from coaching before I was able to understand the truth behind my circumstances. Just like Jonah, the Apostle Paul and so many others who have gone before me, God used my own pride and the pride of others to save my life. If I had stayed at St. John's and continued to be successful, I don't know if my wife would still be alive. I also don't know if I would have ever truly grasped the Gospel and committed my life to Christ.

Pride is a powerful thing. Unchecked, it can exercise control over any given individual. Pride can cause people to covet power. It can drive people to anger. Pride can foster unhealthy bitterness and unforgiveness. Pride is also very deceptive and sneaky. It usually creeps up on us and gradually takes up residence in our minds, our hearts and our souls. I can honestly say that I was guilty of all of the above.

That's why we must be vigilant against any pride that tries to get us off the path God has laid out for us or stop us in our tracks altogether. Here are four ways that we can guard our hearts against the deadly sin of pride and better embrace Christ-like humility:

1. Recognize the pride in your life: Even the most humble people have to deal with pride. We are born with it thanks to the disobedient decision that Adam and Eve made in the Garden of Eden. If you aren't sure about where pride might be lurking or where it is showing up in your life, ask someone you love and trust to give you an honest assessment of any selfish behavior they may have observed. The best way to recognize pride in your life, however, is to ask the Holy Spirit to reveal it to you. He knows you better than you know yourself.

"Search me, O God, and know my heart; test me and know my anxious thoughts. Point out anything in me that offends you, and lead me along the path of everlasting life." (Psalm 139:23-24/NLT)

2. Repent of the pride in your life: Ask God to forgive you of any pride in your life, and then turn away from it. Get rid of it. Stop prideful thoughts from the onset and don't allow them to make their way into your heart.

"Humble yourselves before the Lord, and he will lift you up." (James 4:10/NIV)

3. Reprioritize your life: A great way to shield yourself from pride is to practice putting others first. Find ways to serve your family, your friends, your church and your community. As you reprioritize your life and stop thinking about yourself all the time, it will foster a mindset of humility and help stop pride in its tracks.

"Each of you should use whatever gift you have received to serve others, as faithful stewards of God's grace in its various forms." (1 Peter 4:10/NIV)

4. Recommit to following Jesus' example: While there are many people in our world who are great examples of humility, none can compare to the selflessness Jesus exhibited during His time on Earth. Be intentional in your Bible readings and take time to study the many ways Jesus resisted the temptation to be prideful.

"For even the Son of Man came not to be served but to serve others and to give his life as a ransom for many." (Matthew 20:28/NLT)

Ultimately, getting rid of pride in your life and living with humility is all about surrender. Turning your hopes and dreams and deepest desires to God will allow Him to take over the throne room of your heart. Through prayer and devotion, His Holy Spirit will direct you to live a more humble and less selfish life of purpose and divine fulfillment.

Everybody needs humility.

Study Questions

1. What do you first think of when you hear the word "pride?" What do you first think of when you hear the word "humility?" How would you say modern society has changed the way we think about both of those words?

2. Who are some people you would describe as being humble? What attributes do you think make them that way? How does their humility make them different from others?

3. Can you describe a time when pride got the best of you and caused trouble for yourself and others around you? Were you humbled by the situation? If so, explain what lessons you learned.

4. What are some areas where you feel like you have consistently struggled to resist the temptation of pride? In what ways has pride negatively impacted your relationships?

5. Looking at the four keys to overcoming pride, which ones have you been able to implement in your life? Which ones have you struggled to put into action?

6. What do you need to start doing today that will help you overcome pride? How do you think living with more humility will improve your life and the lives of those around you?

Prayer

Lord, search my heart and reveal to me any prideful thoughts and attitudes I have. Teach me through the example of Christ what it truly means to be humble and selfless. Remind me of the hard lessons that pride has brought my way. Give me the strength to resist the temptation to be proud of my accomplishments and rather give You the glory in everything that You have done through me. Amen.

CHAPTER TWO

UNFINISHED BUSINESS
Everybody Needs To Follow Through

"It was character that got us out of bed, commitment that moved us into action, and discipline that enabled us to follow through." – Zig Ziglar

I loved my dad, and I always will. He was handsome, smart, had a great sense of humor and the gift of gab. If anyone could talk a cat off a fish wagon, it was my dad. My grandparents spoiled my father in an attempt to give him a better life than they had, but unfortunately, they didn't hold him accountable for his actions. They gave him what he wanted, not what he needed. They were always there to bail him out. He never had to work for anything.

My mother loved him and thought he would change when they had a family. Actually, things got worse, because dad had someone in my mom who would work for both of them. To say that dad didn't do right by my mom is an understatement. If he decided to work, which wasn't often, he would spend the money to feed his addiction to alcohol. He rarely had money to support us, so my mom worked two or three jobs. She did her best to make the marriage work, but she was finally forced to get a divorce.

On Fridays, my responsibility was to go find my dad before he would spend whatever money he had made that week. There was a bar on River Street where he used to hang out. If I was fortunate, I'd find him early enough to salvage a little bit of cash. Sometimes it was 10 bucks; sometimes it was 20 dollars. It was never much.

There were many times I found my dad already intoxicated and broke. On those occasions, I would take him back to his apartment, which was down the street from the bar, and put him to bed. Then, I would return home and give my mom very little money, or nothing.

That wasn't the only way my dad let his family down. He loved to fish and hunt, and on many occasions he would tell my brother Stephen and I that he would pick us up and take us fishing.

"Meet me at the corner of Western and Howard at 9 o'clock in the morning," he would say.

When the day finally arrived, Stephen and I would show up with our fishing gear ready to have fun with our dad. But invariably, we would wait and wait and wait. Most of the time, he never showed up. Or if he did show up, it was well after the appointed time. After a while, I stopped waiting and decided to go to the ball field and play baseball with my friends. After that, I never had much of a desire to go fishing. I still don't.

As I became more involved in baseball, my dad would tell me he was going to come to see me play. The fields were literally within 100 yards of his house, but he would never show up. I remember how disappointed I felt and how much I wanted my dad to be a part of my childhood. I think that's why I was so determined to be there at my son Mike's ballgames and my daughter Dana's recitals.

I learned a lot about what a dad was supposed to be by watching what my dad *didn't* do with his family. It was a difficult education in fatherhood, but I took those lessons to heart and tried to make sure I didn't repeat them. It was my responsibility to show my children what being a dad was all about.

Unfulfilled Potential

My dad didn't just have problems following through with promises to his wife and his children. He also had a chronic issue of not following through on the job. He was a master carpenter. He could do anything with his hands. Dad could build a house without a blueprint, but he didn't like to work. He was notorious for starting jobs then not finishing them. I wish my dad had played sports as a youngster because I think he would have learned many valuable lessons about teamwork, hard work, and following through.

Here's how my father operated: He would start a carpentry job and collect the money up front for the materials. Then he would go to the local tavern or race track and blow the money. Next, he would get money for another job and take that money to start working on the job for the first person. This led to a series of unfinished jobs.

People would come to me and say, "Are you Dickie's kid?"

I usually had to ask why they wanted to know. I was afraid that maybe he hadn't finished a job for them or he owed them money. And there wasn't anything I could ever do to help them resolve the issue.

When my father died, I got to speak towards the end of his funeral. I talked about my dad's talent as a carpenter and made light of the fact that when he arrived in Heaven, St. Peter would have all of my dad's unfinished jobs waiting for him to finish. My wife Connie, however, would not be in that line. She would pick him up and make him stay at our house until the job was done. That generated a lot of smiles and laughter from the audience.

I closed by thanking my brother-in-law, Richard Richardson, for the time he spent ministering to my dad during his last days. I wanted everyone to know that my dad had accepted Jesus Christ as his Lord and Savior on the morning of his final day on earth. With that, I heard a resounding "Amen!" from the back of the room.

When I sat down, I thought about how different things could have been for the entire family. Here was a man who had many God-given gifts and abilities, but his lack of desire to work kept him from achieving the greatness for which he had been created. I could have easily hated or resented my dad, but I loved him. At the same time, I felt sorry him.

And God bless my mom. No matter how many times he hurt her or let us down, she always encouraged us to love and respect him, because he was our father.

I never forgot that.

Hidden Talents

Whether it was as a husband, a father or a carpenter, my dad spent his whole life never living up to his full potential. His gifts were sadly wasted, and we didn't get the chance to see what might have been.

Jesus may have been raised in a carpenter's home, but one of His gifts was storytelling. He masterfully weaved timeless truths into relevant subject matter through a series of parables that he shared with His followers.

One of those stories is often referred to as "The Parable of the Talents." Here's the paraphrased version as told in Matthew 25:14-30:

A wealthy man went on a long journey. But before he left, he called three of his servants and gave each some bags of gold (also referred to as talents) to look after while he was gone. He gave five bags to the first servant, two bags to the second servant and one bag to the third servant. While the master was gone, the first servant invested his gold and doubled what he had been given. The second servant did the same. He took his two bags and gained two more. But the third man hid his bag of talents in the ground.

When the wealthy man returned, he was pleased to see that two of his servants had doubled his money.

"Well done, good and faithful servant!" he told both men. "You have been faithful with a few things. I will put you in charge of many things. Come and share your master's happiness!" (vv. 21, 23/NIV)

Then he approached the third servant who had buried the gold in the ground. The servant explained that he was fearful of his master. He knew his master had worked hard for that money and was afraid to lose it.

"You wicked, lazy servant!" the master angrily replied. "You should have put my money on deposit with the bankers, so that when I returned I would have received it back with interest." (vv. 26a, 27/NIV)

The master took the money from the servant and gave it to the one who had 10 bags of gold.

"For whoever has will be given more, and they will have an abundance," the master said. "Whoever does not have, even what they have will be taken from them. And throw that worthless servant outside, into the darkness, where there will be weeping and gnashing of teeth." (vv. 28-30/NIV)

Jesus was explaining through this parable that everyone has been given gifts, abilities and resources. What you do with them will determine what you get back in life. The servants who used the money to make more money were blessed with additional resources and responsibilities, but the servant who was too lazy and afraid to invest his money lost it all.

That third servant was like my dad. He never got as much out of life as he could have, and he found himself on the outside looking in while others reaped the benefits of their hard work and fulfilled potential. Like my dad, I imagine that the third servant had not been taught the value of diligence and what it means to give 100 percent.

As the Apostle Paul wrote, "Whatever you do, do it enthusiastically, as something done for the Lord and not for men." (Colossians 3:23/HCSB)

Everybody Needs To Follow Through

During my career, I coached so many talented players who had incredible God-given ability and potential. Many of them didn't want to do the work that was associated with their talent. They didn't have the internal motivation to follow through.

One of the reasons I pushed my players so hard was because I didn't want their potential to be unfulfilled like my dad's. If anything, I sometimes drove my players a little too hard for that very reason.

On May 8, 2002, former NBA star Allan Iverson famously ranted about practice. Word had gotten out that he had missed practice that season and this had created some tension between him and his head coach, Larry Brown. In the press conference, Iverson used the word "practice" 23 times and tried to make the point that missing one wasn't that big of deal.

Well, practice is essential. Hard work is what allows you to finish what you start and to fulfill your promises. That's how we pay

God back for giving us the gifts He's given us. Whether or not we reach our goals, it's very important that we try to do our best. And that comes from hard work and practice.

Following through with what you've been called to do requires three simple steps:

1. Recognize your talents: We all have gifts and abilities. If you don't know what yours is, seek out some clues based on your personal interests and passions. And if you're still struggling to identify that thing you've been gifted to do, ask someone else to help you discover your hidden talent.

"God has given each of you a gift from his great variety of spiritual gifts. Use them well to serve one another." (1 Peter 4:10a/NLT)

2. Cultivate your talents: Practice makes perfect isn't just a cliché; it's a lifestyle decision. Just because God gave you a talent doesn't mean He is going to do the work for you. He expects you to resist the temptation to be fearful, doubtful or just plain lazy and instead to have the discipline to follow through.

"This is why I remind you to fan into flames the spiritual gift God gave you when I laid my hands on you. For God has not given us a spirit of fear and timidity, but of power, love, and self-discipline." (2 Timothy 1:6-7/NLT)

3. Be faithful with your talents: God gave you gifts and abilities for a purpose. He gave you these things to provide for your family, to make a difference in your community and to bring a message of hope to the world.

"Use (your gift) well to serve one another." (1 Peter 4:10b/NLT)

There is so much potential being left unfulfilled in this world. Think about what would happen if we all recognized our talents, cultivated our talents and were then faithful with our talents and used them for the good of our families, our communities and our world.

Everybody needs to follow through.

Study Questions

1. What are some of your special gifts, talents or abilities? How often and in what ways do you use them?

2. Do you know someone who has unfulfilled potential in his or her life? What issues do you think might be keeping them from being the best they can be?

3. What does the phrase "following through" mean to you? What are some things that keep you from following through in your life?

4. What characteristics did the first two servants in the parable have that allowed them to turn a profit? What characteristics did the third servant have that kept him from doing the same?

5. Of the three keys to fulfilling your potential that were listed, which one(s) have you been able to do well? Which one(s) have you struggled to do?

6. Think about some of the things holding you back from fulfilling your God-given potential. What can you do today that will help you to discover your gifts and use them to their fullest?

Prayer

Lord, I believe that You have blessed me with gifts, abilities and talents. I want to get the most out of what you have given me. I want to use them for the betterment of my family, my community and my world. Give me the courage to step out and do things I've never done before. Give me the self-discipline to cultivate my talents. Give me a faithful heart so that I might use those talents to serve others and bring glory to Your name. Amen.

CHAPTER THREE

STANDING OVATION
Everybody Needs To Be Appreciated

"Make it a habit to tell people thank you, to express your appreciation, sincerely and without the expectation of anything in return. Truly appreciate those around you, and you'll soon find many others around you." – Ralph Marston

"A standing ovation is a form of applause where members of a seated audience stand up while applauding after extraordinary performances of particularly high acclaim." – Wikipedia

You don't know what you've got until it's gone. That statement is more than just a tired cliché. It's a powerful truth that speaks to the increasingly impersonal nature of modern society. Too often, we spend our days in hurry. We get caught up looking to check the next thing off our to do list. We tend to look past the people that make our lives better.

But what happens when those people are gone? If we don't take the time to appreciate them while they are here, we are sadly left with an empty feeling that may never be filled.

It's a lesson that I learned the hard way.

Substitute Dad

My dad, like most of the kids' dads I grew up with, was missing in action. When my mom divorced him, the sole responsibility of raising and providing for the family fell on her shoulders. If it wasn't for my brother Richard, she would not have been able to do it.

Thank God Richard was there for us. He was seven years older than me and literally became my substitute dad. Richard was my best friend, but he was also responsible for disciplining my younger brother, Stephen, and me. There were times when we fought just like most siblings do, but it worked because of how much I loved and respected him.

Richard was handsome and smart. He was the one who was built to play basketball, the game he loved. I often like to kid that he was the white sheep of the family. He was 6-3, weighed about 190 pounds, and had virtually zero body fat. Richard could run. He could jump. He could do it all. But Richard couldn't play in high school because he was the oldest, and he had to work to help my mom support the family.

When Richard graduated from high school, he played with the local semi-pro team. With the help of Rindge Jefferson and the Cambridge Community Center, he was able to earn a basketball scholarship to Jackson State College in Jackson, Mississippi. Unfortunately, he was only able to stay one year because of the financial pressure my mother was under at home. Once again, Richard put family first, came home, and went back to work.

Richard introduced me to the game of basketball and gave me my first ball on my 11th birthday. Not only did he take me to the courts to shoot baskets, but he also took me to my first professional game. It just happened to be Bill Russell's first game with the Celtics. Richard was an avid Celtics fan. By exposing me to the team, he exposed me to legendary head coach Red Auberach, a man who would later become a mentor and a friend.

My dad never made it to any of my basketball or baseball games, but Richard was there as much as possible. He supported me no matter how well I performed or how poorly I did. He came to all of my high school games. Then, when I was playing at Northeastern University and mostly sitting on the bench, Richard would drive as far as 200 miles to see me play a minute or two. When I was disappointed or angry, he would tell me to hang in there and that I had to find a way to make it work.

When I quit the team at Northeastern as a sophomore, Richard hired me to work as a short order cook at his fish and chips restaurant. He also encouraged me to swallow my pride and go back and ask for a second chance, which head coach Dick Dukeshire graciously gave me.

After I became a coach, he would give me honest critiques of how I was doing. He didn't tell me what I wanted to hear. He told me what I needed to hear, and I didn't always like it. Richard would tell me when he thought I was pushing the kids or myself too hard. He knew me better than I knew myself.

I honestly don't know how my life would have turned out if Richard hadn't been there for me during my most formidable years. I do know that I probably wouldn't be writing this book and sharing so many incredible stories, which his hard work afforded me to experience.

Raising The Roof

As he aged, Richard was always in great shape and retained his youthful spirit. I thought my brother and I would grow old together. Perhaps that's why I was so shocked to receive the phone call on December 3, 2002. It was my sister Trudy telling me that Richard had died of a heart attack. I fight back tears every time I think about it. He was only 64 years old.

My wife and I made the trip back to Cambridge for the funeral at St. Paul's AME Church, the same church where we had been married. Richard was my best man on that memorable September day. I was asked to say a few words at his memorial service. I didn't think I could do it, but after asking God for strength, I managed to stand in front of a packed house and talk about my beloved brother.

As I stood behind the pulpit with tears rolling down the side of my face, I reflected on the words that had already been spoken. I was inspired to hear how Richard had mentored and helped so many others. He wasn't the kind of guy to brag about his good deeds, but it was obvious that he had done some incredible work throughout the community.

Toward the end of my speech, I asked everyone to stand. Then, I told the audience that one of the greatest things an athlete can ever receive is a standing ovation. As our home team the Boston Celtics were about to close out a victory, Red Auerbach used to take his starters out of the game, one at a time. As they jogged off the court and headed towards the bench, each one of them, Bill Russell, Bob Cousey, and Satch Sanders, etc., would get a much-deserved standing ovation from the fans.

Because of all he sacrificed, that was the kind of moment that Richard never got to experience.

It wasn't something I had planned to do, but in the moment, I knew what I had to do. Until that point, the gathering had been very somber, but that all changed when I led the entire congregation in a rousing standing ovation for Richard. They clapped, stomped, whistled and yelled so loud and so long it's a wonder that the roof didn't blow off. It completely changed the whole mood from a funeral into a celebration.

To this day, I still regret not telling my brother I loved him more than I did. It was never enough. But I am thankful that I took the opportunity to give my brother Richard his long overdue honor and appreciate him on that bittersweet day.

Everybody Needs To Be Appreciated

It's easy to beat yourself up for not truly appreciating a loved one until they're gone. We've all likely been guilty of taking for granted the people we care for the most. But what if I told you that the same thing happened to a group of men who spent three years with the living, breathing Son of God?

It's true. The disciples that spent every waking hour with Jesus Christ didn't truly appreciate Him for who He was until after He had been crucified on the cross. Some scholars argue that they didn't fully understand His divinity until He rose from the dead three days later. Thankfully for them, they had a second chance to love and appreciate Jesus in the flesh. They also had a precious few days to learn even more from Him as they prepared to build the modern day Christian Church.

That's why it's so important for us to show people how much they mean to use while they're still with us. I can tell you from personal experience how special it is to be on the receiving end of that appreciation. My wife, Connie, was very reluctant to dive into the social media world, but she finally started a Facebook page a few months prior to the writing of this book. I started my own page not long after she did. It has allowed us to reconnect with former players, coaches, family members, and friends. We have found out that we touched a lot of lives. Social media has allowed us to see the impact we've had on others. It's made me realize how important it is to share that same appreciation I've received with those who have had an impact on *my* life.

If you're like me and you haven't always taken the time to appreciate the people around you, here are three simple ways to make that a more regular part of your routine:

1. Don't Wait To Appreciate: There's no better time than the present to share your appreciation. You never know when those people might be gone. Tell them "Thank you," or "I love you" every chance you get. Not only will it lift their spirits, but it will also give you a feeling of joy and completeness. One call, text or letter will not only make their day, but yours as well.

"I always thank my God for you because of His grace given you in Christ Jesus." 1 Corinthians 1:4 (NIV)

2. Don't Be So Selective: Yes, we should love and appreciate the people closest to us. Our family members and our friends should be at the top of that list. But don't stop there. Tell others around you that they have made a difference in your life. Show kindness to a co-worker, a pastor, a coach, or a teacher. It can also be someone you barely know like a waiter or waitress, a store clerk, a traffic cop or the receptionist at your doctor's office. Random acts of appreciation can make someone's day.

"Never let loyalty and kindness leave you! Tie them around your neck as a reminder. Write them deep within your heart." – Proverbs 3:3 (NLT)

3. Don't Drop The Ball: If someone who has impacted your life in a positive way does pass from this life to the next, don't let his or her legacy die. You can carry on the essence of who they were. Live out the lessons you learned from them. Continue their work. Donate to their favorite charity. That is the absolute *best* way that you can honor someone after they are gone.

"Those who are wise will shine like the brightness of the heavens, and those who lead many to righteousness, like the stars for ever and ever." – Daniel 12:3 (NIV)

Now is the time to show love and appreciation. Don't let things like pride, fear or apathy get in the way of making someone else's day better and, at the same time, staving off the kind of guilt and regret that is sure to come otherwise.

Everybody needs to be appreciated.

Study Questions

1. Who are some special people in your life that are no longer alive? Do you feel like you showed them enough appreciation while they were still here?

2. Have you ever been regretful about how much appreciation you have shown a loved one? If so, why do you think that was the case?

2. How do you feel when someone shows appreciation for you? Why do you think appreciation is such an important thing for humans to receive?

3. How often do you think about showing appreciation for people who aren't necessarily family members or close friends? How do you think doing such a thing might have a positive impact on those individuals?

4. Is there anyone whose legacy or commitment to a particular cause you have personally decided to carry now that they are gone? Explain. What are some other ways you might be able to show honor and appreciation for someone after they are gone?

5. What are some things that you can start doing today that will allow you to show greater appreciation for your family members, your close friends and any people (acquaintances or strangers) who have had a positive impact on your life?

Prayer

Lord, help me to be more appreciative of the people You have placed in my life. Help me slow down and recognize the need that they all have for appreciation and honor. Rid my heart of fear, pride and apathy so that I might lift someone up with words of kindness, thankfulness and gratitude. Amen.

CHAPTER FOUR

FAITHFUL TO THE CAUSE
Everybody Needs Commitment

""Commit your works to the Lord and your thoughts will be established." – King Solomon (Proverbs 16:3)

My mother, Dorothy Irene Jarvis, was born on September 15, 1918. As I was writing this book in 2014, she celebrated her 96th birthday. From a very young age, I've always looked at her as a very strong woman. She was a little lady, but she was so strong–physically, emotionally and spiritually.

I experienced my mom's physical strength on one particularly memorable occasion. It was a Saturday at about five o'clock in the afternoon. I was 12 years old at the time, and my younger brother Stephen, who was 10, hadn't come home yet. It was starting to get dark and my mom was getting worried, so she asked me to look for him along the Charles River where he had been fishing.

"I'm not going down there," I defiantly responded. "I'm not his dad."

Needless to say, that was the *wrong* answer. She gave me an old fashioned spanking that I'll never forget. It was the only time my mother had to physically discipline me, but looking back, I certainly deserved it. Besides her faith in God, family was the most important thing in the world to her. That was my little brother she had asked me to find, and she was reminding me that we had to take care of each other, no matter what.

The punishment only lasted for a few moments, but the lesson learned has stayed with me ever since. Commitment isn't always easy, but it's vitally important if you want to save and preserve the most valuable things in your life.

A Mother's Love

My mom raised the family by herself. My dad, a talented carpenter, didn't want to work, so she had to do the work for both of them. She worked at Polaroid during the week and cleaned houses on the weekend so she could provide food, clothes and shelter for her family. Years later, I learned from my older sister Trudy that there were times when my mom would go without food so we could eat.

"She is like the merchant ships, she brings food for her household. She also rises while it is yet night, and provides food for her household." (Proverbs 31:14-15/NKJV)

Most of my clothes were hand-me-downs, but my mother made sure they were always clean and pressed. I probably should have worked at a young age like my older siblings. Instead, my mother gave me the opportunity to go out and play ball with the kids in the neighborhood and pursue athletics to the fullest extent, which made it possible for me to follow my dreams. Only God knows where I would have been if it hadn't been for my mom's unconditional love and commitment.

Mom put up with my dad's lack of financial support, his drinking, and domestic abuse as long as she could, but eventually she had no choice but to divorce him. I think I was eight or nine years old when my dad left and moved in with another woman less than a half mile from our house. Even then, she still encouraged us to love and honor our father in spite of his shortcomings. She made sure that we always remembered his birthday and gave him a Christmas present.

One of the most amazing examples of my mother's commitment to her family took place when my older sister Trudy was a little girl. Trudy was quarantined in the Children's Hospital of Boston for nine months with scarlet fever. During her stay, she had several operations and eventually she lost the ability to hear in her left ear.

After a tiring day at the factory, my mother would walk about a mile to Central Square where she would take the train to Park Street, in the middle of Boston. From there, she would catch a connecting trolley to the hospital. The trip took between an hour and 90 minutes. When my mom arrived, she would stand outside on the sidewalk, praying and waving to her precious little girl as the nurse picked her up in front of the window. Trudy would smile and wave back. My incredible mother battled the cold, the rain and the snow to love on her daughter for about an hour before returning home to feed my brother Stephen and me.

During this incredibly stressful time, my mom became a chain smoker and would go through two to three packs a day. At the end of an exhausting day, she would go to bed with a cigarette in her hand, and before long, there would be a two-inch long drag hanging from the end. One night, some of the ash fell onto the floor and started a fire. Thankfully, the smoke woke her up and she was able to put it out. I'll never forget seeing the burnt rug the next morning, and the terrifying look on my mother's face.

She hugged and kissed Stephen and I as we stood on the rug and thanked God for saving us. She followed with a promise to us that she would stop smoking. Staying true to her word and the commitment that she made to God, herself, and her children, she never smoked again.

My mom was deeply committed to her faith in God. Every Sunday, no matter how tough the week had been or how tired she was, she made sure we got out of bed and got dressed so we could go to church. At the end of the day, every day, my mom would get on her knees in front of her bed. She thanked God for our family and our health, and prayed for our future. Not once did I hear her asking for money, a new house, new clothes, or a car. She was grateful for what God had provided. She is without a doubt the strongest and most committed person I have ever known.

"Her children rise up and call her blessed." (Proverbs 31:28/NLT)

Full Circle

My mom took early retirement at the age of 62. She left Polaroid so she could care for her mother who lived in Fredericton, New

Brunswick, Canada. At least once a month, my mom would gas up her used car and drive 485 miles one way.

Before they had super highways, this incredible woman drove from Waltham, Massachusetts, through New Hampshire, and then through Maine, before crossing the Canadian border. There were very few gas stations along the eight-hour journey. Not once did her car break down. I don't know how she did it, but I do believe that God was with her all the way.

My sister Trudy saw her mother's commitment and took it to heart. When Trudy became a teenager, she made it possible for my mom to work multiple jobs. She performed all of the duties my mother would have usually done. This earned her the title of Associate Head Mother. My brother Steve later upgraded Trudy to Sr. Associate Head Mother.

My mom's commitment came full circle when she was no longer able to adequately take care of herself. Trudy refused to put her into a retirement home. Instead, she and her husband Reggie graciously and compassionately moved mom into their home in Maryland.

The Staggering Cost

Throughout the ages, there have been countless individuals who have displayed uncommon levels of commitment for many a cause. Biblical figures such as Abraham, David, Esther and the Apostle Paul, along with American heroes such as Harriet Tubman, Martin Luther King and Billy Graham, have inspired us to learn and embrace the true meaning of faithfulness.

However, for those of us within the Christian faith, there is undeniably one person who stands above everyone else when it comes to commitment. That person is Jesus Christ.

According to the New Testament, when Jesus came to earth, He left His Father's side in Heaven. He humbled himself and lived as a man. Even though He had access to all of the riches in glory, Jesus was born into a simple life with little material wealth. When He started His ministry, the Jewish elite rebuffed Him and His own people rejected Him because they thought He was common, like them.

Jesus did all of this despite knowing the staggering cost of His commitment. In the end, He was mocked, convicted of a crime that He didn't commit, brutally tortured, and hung naked on a cross to die. A short while later, Jesus' disciples followed His example and courageously laid the foundation for the early Christian church while performing miracles and sharing the Gospel (the Good News), even in the face of persecution and martyrdom.

According to various historical reports, 11 of the 12 disciples, now known as Apostles, were martyred for their faith. Andrew, Nathanael, Peter, Philip, Thaddeus and Simon were crucified. James, the son of Zebedee, was executed with a sword. James, son of Alphaeus, was thrown to his death from the Temple wall. Thomas was speared. Matthew was beheaded. Matthias, a replacement for Judas Iscariot, who betrayed Jesus and then committed suicide, was stoned while hanging on a cross. Only John died a natural death.

Think for a moment about what our families, our cities, our nation, and our world would be like if we all had the same level of commitment that Jesus and His disciples modeled for us.

Everybody Needs Commitment

Commitment is a powerful thing. Just as the previous stories conveyed, it takes commitment to save and preserve the things that are most valuable to us. For my mom, it was about saving her family. For Jesus and His disciples, it was all about saving the world.

Sadly, today's world is lacking in commitment. Faithful and consistent living is no longer expected and is decreasingly put into practice. This has led to the deterioration of the family, the corruption of government, and the moral collapse of society.

If you're like me and you want to protect your family and make a difference in your community and see lives changed throughout this world, it's going to take a greater understanding of what it means to truly be committed:

1. Find A Cause: What are you passionate about? Is it your family? Is it your church? Is it your community? Is it a societal issue?

When our passions are lined up with God's will, then those are usually the things at which we excel and the things to which we will be the most committed. You may not always feel like God has called you to a particular cause, but His word says otherwise:

"For we are God's handiwork, created in Christ Jesus to do good works, which God prepared in advance for us to do." (Ephesians 2:10/NIV)

2. Understand The Purpose: What is the greater purpose behind the cause? Regardless of the cause to which you attach yourself, make sure that it matters to God. Our cause and the purpose behind it should be aligned with His Word and have a biblical view, not the world's view.

"Therefore, my brothers and sisters, make every effort to confirm your calling and election. For if you do these things, you will never stumble, and you will receive a rich welcome into the eternal kingdom of our Lord and Savior Jesus Christ." (2 Peter 2:10-11/NIV)

3. Build A Team: Just as a warrior can't go into battle alone and expect to win the fight, you must find others who are equally committed to the cause if you will have any chance for success. Surround yourself with those people and work together for the greater good.

"Two people are better off than one, for they can help each other succeed. If one person falls, the other can reach out and help. But someone who falls alone is in real trouble. Likewise, two people lying close together can keep each other warm. But how can one be warm alone? A person standing alone can be attacked and defeated, but two can stand back-to-back and conquer. Three are even better, for a triple-braided cord is not easily broken." (Ecclesiastes 4:9-12/NLT)

4. Be Prepared To Sacrifice: Count the cost. Know exactly what you might have to sacrifice in order to see the mission through to its completion. This could mean separating yourself from those slowing you down or diverting your attention. There could be a financial sacrifice involved. It could mean walking away from another dream. And in some cases, sacrifice could mean putting yourself in the crosshairs of persecution or even life threatening situations.

"Then He said to them all, if anyone would come after me, he must deny himself, and take up his cross daily, and follow me." (Luke 9:23/NIV)

5. Don't Waver: Commitment means staying the course, no matter what challenges come your way. In those times when it might be easier to take a less difficult path, know that God has given you His Holy Spirit to strengthen and encourage you.

"This is my command—be strong and courageous! Do not be afraid or discouraged. For the Lord your God is with you wherever you go." (Joshua 1:9/NLT)

6. Give It All To God: Sometimes it's easy for us to get caught up in the good things we're trying to do and forget that it's really not about us. When we give everything to God, however, it makes it so much easier to win the battle within our own minds. Commitment isn't such a difficult proposition when we fully understand to whom we're committing and why. God will give us the emotional fortitude and mental strength to overcome any temptations to give up.

"Commit your works to the Lord and your thoughts will be established." (Proverbs 16:3/NKJV)

Making the decision to stay committed to your family, to your faith in Christ and to whatever mission you have been called is the easy part. But following through and resisting the temptation to give up when things get tough? That's the hard part. In the end, only those who are fully committed will enjoy the fruits of their labor and hear these words one day:

"Well done, good and faithful servant!" (Matthew 25:21/NIV)

Everybody needs commitment.

Study Questions

1.What are some things to which you are committed? How would you rank those things in order of importance?

2. What are some things that challenge your commitment in certain areas?

3. Why do you think it can be so easy to waver on some commitments?

4. Do you feel like you know what your primary callings are in life? Does knowing that make it easier or more difficult to stay committed?

5. Of the five keys to commitment listed, which ones have you been the most successful at living out? With which of those keys have you struggled?

6. What are some things you can start doing today that will help you to stay more committed to God's purposes for your life?

Prayer

Lord, reveal to me Your perfect purpose for my life. Help me to stay committed to the cause and not allow challenges and difficulties to take me off the path. Give me the strength and the courage to be Your vessel no matter the cost, no matter what I might have to sacrifice along the way. Amen.

CHAPTER FIVE

KEEP SWINGING
Everybody Needs Determination

"If at first you don't succeed, try, try, try again." – *Thomas H. Palmer*

One of the most influential people in my life was my first baseball coach, Stretch Headley. One quick glance and it was obvious how he got his nickname. Stretch was 6-7 at a time when six-feet was considered tall. He played first base and possessed the wingspan of a seven-footer. He could seemingly stretch across the diamond and pluck the ball out of the third baseman's hand. Twenty-two years later, I would coach his son Kevin.

I will never forget the first time I met Stretch. It was on my 10th birthday when I was walking across Hoyt Field on the way to the basketball courts to shoot some hoops with the ball that my brother Richard had just given me for my birthday.

"Crisco!" Stretch yelled. "Crisco! C'mon over here!"

I was a husky kid, but I ran as quickly as I could to see what Stretch wanted.

"Do you wanna play for my baseball team?" he asked.

That was an easy question to answer. Of course I did. I jumped at the opportunity to play with some of my neighborhood buddies on my first real team. What I didn't realize at the time was that Stretch only had eight boys and needed a ninth to complete the team. All the positions were filled except one. Stretch needed a catcher and on most little league teams, the little fat kid usually filled that position. And that little fat kid happened to be me.

Stretch sent me over to home plate where a mask, a chest protector, a catcher's mitt and two shin pads were waiting for me. I'll never forget the first time I put them on and crouched down behind the plate. I could barely move and hardly see. In hindsight, I can honestly say that my first day as a catcher was the beginning of my coaching career because I became the coach on the field. I enjoyed telling the players where they should move and the pitcher what pitches he should throw. I was the boss of the diamond, and I loved it.

With practice I became a pretty good catcher. If I could have hit the curve ball more often I might have had a career in baseball. But no matter how many times I swung and missed, Stretch would encourage me to keep swinging.

"You're never gonna hit the ball if you don't swing at it," he said. "If you strike out, go down swingin' and do it with style."

Although I did my best to take that message to heart, most of the time my fear and doubt got the best of me. I remember one game in particular like it was yesterday. I had been missing the ball miserably, and some of the guys were making fun of me. Late in the game, we were down by two runs and had two men on base. It was my turn at bat.

When I walked up to the plate, I was feeling sorry for myself and just knew I was going to strike out. Just before the pitcher began his wind up I started to cry and could barely see. Thank God I could hear the voice of my coach telling me to "keep swinging" as the pitcher moved his arm toward home plate. I gripped the bat as tight as I could, closed my eyes, took a deep breath to calm myself, and swung as hard as I could.

I never saw the ball, but I did hear the distinct cracking sound when the ball made solid contact with the bat. When I opened my eyes, I couldn't believe what I was seeing. It was the best hit of my little league career. The ball went sailing between the leftfielder and the centerfielder. My teammates scored, and I hustled around the bases for an inside the park home run. As I crossed home plate, I was mobbed by my teammates and Stretch, who lifted me up and put me on his shoulders.

I gained a lot of confidence that day, and it carried over into other aspects of my life. That might not have happened if I had not been able to overcome my fears and doubts and kept swinging.

Keep Shooting

Basketball coaches have different philosophies on how to handle a player who isn't shooting well. I always wanted my better shooters to never pass up a good shot and believed that every shot they took was going in the basket.

That was the case with a kid named Elijah Ingram. He was a McDonald's All-American from Jersey City, New Jersey, where he played for St. Anthony High School and Hall of Fame coach Bob Hurley Sr.

Elijah was a 5-10 lefty who not only could handle the ball well, but he was also an excellent three-point shooter. During the 2002-03 season when I was the head basketball coach at St. John's University, he started right away as a freshman and finished as the team's leader in three pointers (70) and three-point shooting percentage (.361), and was the second leading scorer (10.5).

However, on February 18, 2003, something interesting happened in the heat of the Big East Conference regular season that threatened this rising star's confidence. We traveled upstate for a game against Syracuse and head coach Jim Boeheim. The Orangemen featured a freshman named Carmelo Anthony and would eventually win the national championship.

In typical fashion, the Carrier Dome was packed with over 20,000 fans, but the noise level was the least of my concerns. It was Boeheim's signature 2-3 zone that gave our team the most trouble. Elijah missed his first three attempts from behind the arc. Coach Boeheim could see that he wasn't shooting with confidence and told his defenders to play off of him. This left Elijah even more open. The more open he was, the more he missed, and the less he wanted to shoot.

I called a couple of timeouts and told him that he had to keep shooting. If he didn't, I would put him on the bench. I knew how much he wanted to be on the court, so Elijah did as he was told and ended up shooting 10 percent on two for 20 shooting in a tough and disappointing 66-60 loss.

After the game, Lenny Robbins from the *The New York Post* interviewed Elijah about the game and his performance. I almost fell off my chair when Elijah told Lenny that it was my fault because I told him to keep shooting. On the ride home, Elijah and I had a heart-to-heart talk about the game and my decision to have him keep shooting. Thank God I did, because Elijah realized how much faith and confidence I had in him. He never questioned me again.

Elijah's shooting touch returned and thanks in large part to his three point shooting, we finished the regular season on a three-game winning streak, including a huge upset of Duke. A few weeks later, I watched Elijah and the rest of the team climb the ladder to cut down the nets after we defeated Georgetown to win the National Invitational Tournament (NIT) in Madison Square Garden.

On A Mission

Moses was one of the greatest leaders of all times and was asked by God to lead the Israelites out of slavery in Egypt. Moses told God that he wasn't the right man for the job because he thought his people would reject him and because he wasn't a good speaker. God told Moses that He would provide him with everything he needed including his brother, Aaron, who would act as his spokesman. Eventually, Moses courageously followed God's voice and famously guided his people to freedom (Exodus 12-14).

When his days were over, another great man named Joshua filled the void and was divinely chosen to take the helm and lead the people into The Promised Land (Deuteronomy 31:1-8). The biblical account describes how Joshua and the Israelites crossed the Jordan River into Canaan where they came upon the powerful city of Jericho and its impenetrable walls. But God promised Joshua that nothing would stand in his way. Jericho would be defeated as long as he and the Israelites followed the Lord's instructions.

"March around the city once with all the armed men. Do this for six days. Have seven priests carry trumpets of rams' horns in front of the ark. On the seventh day, march around the city seven times, with the priests blowing the trumpets. When you hear them sound a long blast on the trumpets, have the whole army give a loud shout; then the wall of the city will collapse and the army will go up, everyone straight in." (Joshua 6:3-5)

From a tactical standpoint, this must have seemed like a ridiculous plan. How would marching around a city for seven days and then blowing some trumpets bring down such famously fortified walls? Surely the people thought that Joshua had gone mad. But they listened to and followed their leader's instructions perfectly. Just as God had parted the Red Sea to allow the Israelites to escape Pharaoh's army, He brought down those walls at the sound of His people's obedient shout.

The Bible also tells us about Naaman, an Aramean army commander who suffered from the painful skin disease of leprosy (2 Kings 5:1-14). Naaman reached out to a powerful prophet named Elisha, who had a reputation for performing miracles in God's name. Elisha responded with an unusual letter. He told Naaman to wash himself seven times in the Jordan River. This made no sense. How could swimming around in an unclean body of water cure him of leprosy? Naaman pridefully rejected Elisha's advice.

But Naaman's servants talked sense into their master and convinced him to do as the prophet suggested. After dipping himself in the Jordan seven times, "his flesh was restored and became clean like that of a young boy" (2 Kings 5:14).

In both of these stories, the people involved were given a choice: have the faith to do something unconventional that might make them look foolish, or give in to fear, doubt and pride, and fall short of the victory.

Naaman's and Joshua's circumstances were very different, but both men had to truly believe that God's plans would work and not worry about what others might think. They both had a mission and reaped the rewards that come from not giving up.

Everybody Needs Determination

When I was a little league baseball player, I was determined to do my best, make my coach proud, and help my team win. As a coach, I wanted my players–including Elijah Ingram–to have that same kind of determination and never give up, even when the odds were against them or they might look a little foolish.

One of the greatest examples of determination can be found in the New Testament. Some men came carrying a paralyzed man on a mat so that Jesus could heal him. They tried to get to Jesus, but they couldn't push through the crowd. So they went up to the roof, took off some of the tiles and lowered the sick man, who was still on the mat in front of Jesus. Seeing their faith and determination, Jesus told the paralyzed man to "Stand up, pick up your mat, and walk!" (John 5:8/NIV).

They were determined to do what was necessary to help their friend. They weren't worried about how they looked to those around them. All that mattered was that their friend got the healing he so desperately needed.

In life, we have to keep swinging. We have to keep shooting. We have to keep marching. We have to keep seeking. We have to keep praying. We have to be willing to go the distance. If we don't try, we will never succeed.

Whatever your mission in life is, whether it's a daily charge or a lifelong goal, God will give you the strength and determination you need to fight through disappointments and not succumb to fear, doubt, or pride, even if that means looking a little foolish along the way.

Everybody needs determination.

Study Questions

1. Can you think of a time when you were asked to do something purposeful that seemed a little foolish at the time? Did you go through with it? If so, what was the result?

2. How often do doubt, fear, or pride keep you from finishing your designated tasks?

3. Why do you think pride is such a strong enemy of determination? What other factors tend to work against our determination to complete important tasks?

4. Think back to the Bible stories referenced in this chapter (Moses, Joshua, Naaman, and the paralyzed man we read about in Luke). Can you relate to any of these stories? How might the determination these individuals displayed help you fulfill your purpose in life?

5. What are some ways that you can encourage others to be more determined to achieve their goals?

6. Can you name one thing you are determined to accomplish today? This week? This month? This year?

Prayer

Lord, I know you have a plan and a purpose for my life. Help me to see that plan clearly. Give me the strength and determination to fight through the fear, doubt and prideful thoughts that might keep me from completing that mission. I trust You completely, and I will faithfully follow You along this path to victory. Amen.

CHAPTER SIX

WHEN GOD LAUGHS
Everybody Needs A Plan

"Man plans. God laughs." – Yiddish Proverb

From a very young age, I knew I wanted to be a coach. However, it wasn't until I reached college that I started to formulate a plan as to how my dream might become a reality. The goal was to become the head boy's varsity basketball coach at my alma mater– Cambridge Rindge and Latin High School. Once there, I was going to develop a national program like powerhouse DeMatha Catholic High School in Washington D.C., where all of the players earned scholarships to play college basketball.

My quest began after I graduated from Northeastern University in 1968. The plan was to apply for a physical education job at the high school and secure an assistant coaching position. I managed to get the teaching position, but I was unable to get the junior varsity basketball job for which I applied. I didn't get the freshman basketball job either. Instead, I received coaching positions on the football and baseball staffs.

I just *knew* that the rest of my plan was right around the corner, but it wasn't.

As I waited for the opportunity to come, my college coach Dick Dukeshire offered me the opportunity to work as his assistant at Northeastern. I spent the next five years there, including one season with future Hall of Fame coach Jim Calhoun during his first year at the helm. From there, I went to Harvard University where I assisted legendary Boston Celtics player Tom "Satch" Sanders for another four years. For nine years, I taught P.E. during the day, coached college basketball in the evening, and coached high school baseball in the offseason.

I began to feel that I was never going to land my dream job. I decided it was time to set my sights on a college head coaching position. That same year, in 1977, Satch was offered a coaching job with the Celtics, and I was sure that I was going to be the next coach at Harvard. After a three-month wait, I received the dreaded phone call and was told that the university was going to hire Frank McLaughlin, who had served as Digger Phelps' assistant at Notre Dame.

After hanging up, I went upstairs, stretched out across the bed and began to cry like a baby. My wife Connie came into our bedroom and wrapped her arms around me as tears streamed down my face. What she said didn't make much sense to me at the time.

"Don't worry Mike," she said. "God's got something better in mind."

I couldn't imagine what that "something better" might be.

As King Solomon once wrote, "How can we understand the road we travel? It is the Lord who directs our steps." (Proverbs 20:24/NLT)

The following year, I continued teaching and coaching other sports at the high school. Tim Mahoney, a good friend of mine, was the head boys' varsity basketball coach. His team had a fantastic season but fell short with a loss in the semifinals to the eventual state champion. That wasn't good enough for the Cambridge community and Tim's contract was not renewed.

In a strange twist, some of the basketball program's boosters and two of my dearest friends, Lenny Johnson and Paul Chase, took up a petition to hire me as the new head coach. After 10 years of waiting and a school committee meeting that lasted until two in the morning, I got the job thanks to a razor thin 4-3 vote.

When I heard the news, I remembered what my wife told me on that summer night the year before when I didn't get the head job at Harvard. As usual, she was right. God *did* have something better in mind and that included me getting the dream job, which allowed me to coach future NBA Hall of Fame center Patrick Ewing, All-American Rumeal Robinson, and a lot of other great kids.

During my seven years as the head coach, we won three consecutive state championships, earned a #1 national ranking, and built one of the top high school basketball programs in the nation. All but two of my players went on to institutions of higher learning. One became a policeman, the other a fireman.

It wasn't exactly as I planned. It was better, and definitely worth the wait. As Solomon again wisely wrote, "You can make plans, but the Lord's purpose will prevail." (Proverbs 19:21/NLT)

God's Trump Card

It might be cliché, but history certainly has a way of repeating itself.

In 2008, after five years away from coaching, I accepted an offer to lead the basketball program at Florida Atlantic University in Boca. My son Mike Jr., who had been a member of the Duke basketball staff, gave up a lucrative position with Marquis Jet to work side by side with me as my associate head coach. The last time we had worked together was during the 2002-03 season at St. John's.

Mike Jr. and I were going to build a winning program at Florida Atlantic and bring big time college basketball to Boca Raton. My plan was to serve as the head coach for seven years and then turn it over to my son at the end of the 2014-15 season. He would become the head coach and I would become *his* assistant. I thought it would be a great way to end my career; a great plan with a storybook ending!

That was *my* plan. But God had others plans.

Building a winning basketball program at FAU would be more difficult than expected. We won a total of six games in our first year, 14 in year two, and then we put it all together in the third year posting a record of 21-11, which would earn us the SunBelt Conference regular season championship and a trip to the National Invitational Tournament (NIT), all firsts for FAU. That championship year was followed by two sub-500 seasons, a lot of close losses, another first round defeat in the conference tournament, and a new athletic director who questioned my age and made it known that he wanted his own guy.

When we met for an evaluation at the end of my fifth year, I knew my days were numbered. He told me my greatest weakness was that I cared more about my players than they cared about themselves. Mike Jr., and I would coach our last game together in a tough loss to Marshall University in the first round of the 2014 Conference USA tournament in El Paso.

April 30, 2014 was my last official day at FAU. I was out, and there was no program to hand over to my son.

But God knew what He is doing. He doesn't make mistakes. He knew it was time for me to end my coaching career and transition into the next phase of my life. Like my wife told me the night I didn't get the job at Harvard, God had something better in mind. He wanted me to begin writing this book a year earlier than I planned so that I could begin to speak into the lives of coaches, athletes and parents.

At first I thought I had been dealt a bad hand, but once again I'm thankful that God trumped *my* plans with His.

In God's Time

Our plans usually go awry for one of two reasons. Either we are trying to implement a plan that doesn't line up with God's, or we get impatient and try to hurry things up. In the Old Testament case of Abraham and his wife Sarah, both of those mistakes were made.

Abraham, at that time known as Abram, was living in the Chaldean city of Ur (in what is now modern day Iraq) when God called him to leave his homeland. He promised Abraham that he would become the father of many nations (Genesis 12:1-3). But Sarah, then known as Sarai, was unable to bear children. How could her husband be the father of a great nation if he had no descendents of his own?

After 10 years of waiting, Sarah came up with her own plan. She would allow Abraham to have a child with her Egyptian servant

Hagar (Genesis 16:1-3). This decision caused great tension in Abraham's household, but the plan seemingly worked when Hagar gave birth to a son named Ishmael.

But as King Solomon would write in the future: "Human plans, no matter how wise or well advised, cannot stand against the Lord." (Proverbs 21:30/NLT)

Four years later, God spoke to Abraham again.

"I am El-Shaddai–'God Almighty.' Serve me faithfully and live a blameless life. I will make a covenant with you, by which I will guarantee you countless descendents." (Genesis 17:1-2/NLT)

It was during this encounter when God gave him the name Abraham and promised him that one seed of his descendants would be the Savior of all mankind. Then God added:

"Regarding Sarai, your wife, her name will no longer be Sarai, from now on you will call her Sarah. And I will bless her richly, and she will become the mother of many nations. Kings will be among her descendants!" (Genesis 17:16/NLT)

Abraham bowed down to the ground and laughed to himself in disbelief.

"How can I become a father at a hundred years old?" he wondered. "And Sarah is ninety! How can *she* have a baby?"

It didn't make sense in the natural, but a year later Abraham and Sarah welcomed their son Isaac into the world just as God had promised. (Genesis 21:1-7)

Isaac's birth represented more than just God's faithfulness. It represented the birth of a powerful nation. Because Abraham and Sarah were impatient and took matters into their own hands, however, there was also great consequence. Ishmael's descendents would grow in number and strength, and from his ancestral line came the Islam religion. Ishmael's people have been in conflict with the rest of the world ever since, just as God had promised (Genesis 16:12).

Like Abraham and Sarah, we often take matters into our own hands. We try to make things happen before their time or we try to force *our* plans on God. And sometimes, we don't have a plan at all and walk aimlessly searching for purpose. In each of those situations, there are consequences we eventually face when our plans don't line up with His.

Everybody Needs A Plan

As I was working my way through the coaching ranks, I leaned heavily on attorney Rob Ades to help me navigate contract negotiations and employment transitions. It was from Rob that I first heard an old Yiddish Proverb that has been passed down throughout the ages. As he liked to say, "We make plans. God laughs."

Does God really laugh at us when we make plans for our life? Maybe not. But I can't help wonder if He isn't somewhat amused when we think we've got it all figured out. I envision God shaking His head with a smile on His face as He watches us work so hard to make things happen. God does not want us to wait around expecting others to give us what we want. He wants us to pray for His assistance. If it agrees with His plan, it will be done just as Jesus established when He taught the disciples the Lord's Prayer (Matthew 6:9-13).

How much easier would our lives be if we could only understand some simple biblical truths about *God's* plan?

1. Everybody needs a plan: It doesn't matter whether we're talking about business, family, ministry, sports or even recreation. No venture ever succeeds without a plan.

"Good planning and hard work lead to prosperity, but hasty shortcuts lead to poverty." (Proverbs 21:5/NLT)

2. God has a plan for us: This is the next step in the right direction. We must acknowledge the fact that God created us for a purpose, and His plan is a good plan.

"For I know the plans I have for you," says the LORD. "They are plans for good and not for disaster, to give you a future and a hope." (Jeremiah 29:11/NLT)

3. God's plan might be different than our plan: Most of the time, our plans are based on what *we* want and not what *He* wants.

And even when our plans seem to be good, if they aren't from God, they will never truly fulfill us.

"Many are the plans in a man's heart, but it is the Lord's purpose that prevails." (Proverbs 19:21/NIV)

4. God's plan has perfect timing: This is one of the hardest things for us as humans to accept. Patience is not a trait that typically comes naturally for us. It's very easy to want to rush things along even when we're carrying out the plan God has laid out for us. But we can't see everything that He sees. It's always best to wait and never get ahead of God.

"For still the vision awaits its appointed time; it hastens to the end–it will not lie. If it seems slow, wait for it; it will surely come; it will not delay." (Habakkuk 2:3/ESV)

5. God's plan is bigger and better than our plan: Perhaps you've planned on becoming the President of the United States or a professional athlete or a famous entertainer. Those are pretty big plans. But God's plan is always bigger and better. It's bigger because it goes beyond what our minds can conceive. His plan stretches into eternity. And it's better because it's always what is *best* for us–not what *we* think is best.

"No eye has seen, no ear has heard, and no mind has imagined what God has prepared for those who love him." (1 Corinthians 2:9/NLT)

6. We all have the same plan: Certainly our paths are very different and our stations in life will vary greatly, but God's primary purpose and plan for each of us can be found in the Bible, or as I like to call it, "God's Playbook."

"The most important commandment is this: 'Listen, O Israel! The Lord our God is the one and only Lord. And you must love the Lord your God with all your heart, all your soul, all your mind, and all your strength.' The second is equally important: 'Love your neighbor as yourself.' No other commandment is greater than these." (Matthew 12:29-31/NLT)

Working out God's plan for our lives is about understanding how everything is connected back to Him. It's all about God. It's not about you. It's not about me. It's about letting *His* will be done. It's about us using the gifts that *He* has given us—not for our glory, but for His glory.

One thing is certain. If you don't have a plan or if you haven't submitted to God's plan for your life, you aren't going anywhere anytime soon. You might have some success according to this world's definition of the word, but you will ultimately find yourself pressing and struggling to stay ahead. There's no real joy in that. There's no real purpose either.

But God's plan is perfect. It's fulfilling. It has purpose. It's better than anything you can ever imagine.

Everybody needs a plan.

Study Questions

1. Do you feel like God has a plan for your life? If so, what do you think that plan is?

2. Of the three stories discussed (Coach Jarvis waiting for the Cambridge job, Coach Jarvis making plans at FAU, and Abraham and Sarah waiting to have a child), which one resonated most with you?

3. When have you been impatient with God's plan? Why was it hard to wait? Can you think of a time when you were patient and waited on the Lord? How did that situation turn out?

4. Can you think of a time when you were outside of God's plan or had different ideas about what God's plan was for your life? What happened in that situation and what, if any, consequences did you face?

5. Can you think of a time when you didn't know the plan? How did that affect your everyday life? Did you eventually discover God's plan?

6. At this time in your life, do you have any plans you need to change? Read Proverbs 16:3. What are some things you can do today that will allow you to commit your work to the Lord and align your plans with His?

Prayer

Lord, I acknowledge that I need Your plan for my life. I am lost without You. I need Your direction. Give me the patience to wait for Your perfect plan to unfold. Give me the courage to walk through Your plan no matter what difficult circumstances might come my way. Help me get rid of any plans that don't line up with Your plans so that I might fulfill the greater purpose that You have for my life. Amen.

CHAPTER SEVEN

SILENT PARTNER
Everybody Needs A General Manager

"Two people are better off than one, for they can help each other suc-ceed." – King Solomon (Ecclesiastes 4:9/NIV)

If it wasn't for my wife Connie, I wouldn't have much of a story to tell.

It took me 60 years to be born again, but God has always been first in her life. She accepted Christ at a Billy Graham crusade held inside the Boston Garden when she was 12 years old. A lot of the kids I taught in high school were in the Sunday School class that she taught at St. Paul's A.M.E. Church in Cambridge. And when we got married, she was the spiritual rock in our family and made sure we were connected to God and His Word. Wherever my coaching career took us, the first thing she insisted was that we find a church home.

Even as I was figuring out what it really meant to be a follower of Christ, my wife was setting an incredible example for me and for our kids. She was the shining light, the encouraging silent partner who held everything together and allowed me to pursue my dreams.

I truly believe that God put us together, and because of His love, we were able to stay together.

The Girl (Right) Next Door

The summer before I started ninth grade, our family moved four blocks, from Howard Street to River Street. It turned out to be the shortest but most significant move of my life. That's where I met Cornelia Anne Gordon.

At first, Connie was just the girl next door. Then we became friends. We took long walks along the Charles River and ended our days talking on the telephone. Next, we became high school sweethearts and attended each other's senior proms.

"What are you two doing on the phone?" my mom would always say. "Just open the window!"

The separation between our two houses couldn't have been more than 15 feet, so when the phone wasn't free, we would meet on Connie's front steps and talk for hours.

When we first started dating in high school, Connie didn't know that much about basketball, but she decided to learn so she could spend more time with me. As we got more serious in our relationship, Connie made the decision that she would support me in my career pursuits.

We got married in our early 20s, and by then my coaching career was already in motion. Connie didn't try to become a master technician of basketball. Instead, she decided that she would use her God-given gifts and skills to help me. Thanks to her mother, affectionately known as Nana Hurley, Connie was a great cook. She knew that the best way to reach a man's heart is through his stomach. Connie, like her mother, took great pride in everything she did. When she cooked for the team, it was as if she was cooking for the Lord.

I have a bachelor's degree and a master's degree, but as I've said on more than one occasion, both of our names should be on those degrees. When I was in college, Connie typed and edited my papers. She helped me study for my exams. While I was coaching at Boston University, Connie went back to school and earned her undergraduate degree from Emmanuel College. She was then accepted into a prestigious counseling program at BU, but when I accepted the job at George Washington University, she put her career on hold so I could continue to pursue mine.

Two years later, Connie returned to school and earned a master's degree in counseling from GWU. She used her newfound knowledge to assist me behind the scenes. Connie attended practice and studied the players' body language, their attitudes, their communication skills, their reactions to criticism, their ability to lead, their ability to follow, their work ethic, and their commitment to making the team better. She made it possible for me to have a better understanding of my players and the issues they were facing.

It's almost impossible to do your job well unless you have a healthy marriage. As they say, "Happy wife, happy life." Connie embraced her role as a mother and wife, but she also enjoyed helping me with my job. She felt that by assisting me, Team Jarvis could make a positive difference in our players' lives and help direct their futures.

I often referred to her as my general manager. Connie traveled to almost all the games. She became an integral part of the program, sometimes the most *important* part. She was the glue that held our team and our family together. Over time, Connie also became very knowledgeable about basketball, so much so that she started to worry me a little bit.

"Let me show you a play," she sometimes suggested. Then she would smile.

During the tumultuous times at St. John's, things got a little rough for my family, and it was hard for Connie not to take things personal. Somehow she was able to put her game face on and take the heat. At one point during the 2002-03 season, one of my starters had a girlfriend who wasn't happy about his role. She took it upon herself to do something about it. From her seat in the stands she started a chant:

"Fi-re Jar-vis! Fi-re Jar-vis!"

After a while, it became uncomfortable for Connie to sit in the stands behind our bench. It was hard to enjoy the games with such unkind words showering from the peanut gallery. Toward the end of our time in New York, Josephine Trana at Madison Square Garden arranged for Connie to sit alone in one of the skyboxes high above the court. Although it had become too difficult to hear the booing and the negative remarks that were being directed at me, she felt like she had to be there.

Most importantly, it was her fervent prayers and an unwavering commitment to her faith that caused my heart to turn more and more toward God in a significant, life-changing way.

Noah's Better Half

Not many Old Testament figures stand more prominently than Noah. His story has been told and retold countless times. The details of the ark's construction and the subsequent Great Flood have been discussed and debated throughout the ages. But curiously, we know very little about Noah's wife.

In the Genesis account (Genesis 6-9), her name is not given although some theologians, and many within the Jewish tradition, believe she might have been Naamah, a woman who was briefly mentioned in Adam's genealogy (Genesis 4:22). And that's what makes her so interesting. Anyone who is married knows that a man like Noah could not have spent an estimated 100 years building a gargantuan boat without some serious backing from his better half.

Think about it. Not only did Noah's wife have to agree that her husband was doing God's work, she also had to take care of the little things that happened behind the scenes, like making sure everyone was fed, making sure the house was in order, taking care of the children, and providing emotional support throughout the process.

Considering the wickedness that ran rampant at the time, there's a strong likelihood Noah was mocked relentlessly while building the ark. This would have been painful for his wife to watch. After all, her sons were also helping their father, and any vicious verbal attacks would have been an affront to the family she was committed to serving and protecting. It might have been easy for Noah's wife to get frustrated and want her husband to quit working on such a ridiculous project, but she stood firm and continued to encourage him to keep going. Sounds familiar.

And then there was the matter of the flood itself. Before the rain began to fall, God told Noah to gather seven pairs of clean animal and two pairs of every other kind of animal (Genesis 6:19-20). No one knows for sure how many animals were on the ark, but the estimates usually range between 5,000 and 50,000 creatures that shared space with Noah and his family. I can't think of too many wives that would be terribly excited about 360 days on a boat with that kind of living arrangement.

Noah's wife must have trusted in her husband, and no doubt she trusted in God. That's what made her such an effective silent partner. I can't imagine Noah could have succeeded in this daunting task without someone incredibly strong and courageous standing at his side.

Everybody Needs A General Manager

In the world of professional sports, there is perhaps no more important job than that of the general manager. As the team's top executive, the GM makes some of the biggest decisions regarding player personnel (signing free agents, selecting players in a draft, etc.), the hiring and firing of coaches, and the negotiation and execution of contracts.

But unlike managers, coaches and players, the GM is often pulling strings behind the scenes and not nearly as public and out front as other key members of the team. This has changed somewhat over the years as media reporting and fan scrutiny has intensified. Still, for the most part, a team's GM acts more like a silent partner than the lead dog.

When I was coaching, I needed someone to act as my general manager, and that person was my wife Connie. She kept my life in order and allowed me to dive head first into my job as a head coach. Likewise, Noah needed his wife to handle his personal affairs so that he could stay focused and complete the task at hand.

Even Jesus needed a general manager. Though He was the Son of God, He too had someone working on his behalf. Not only was Jesus' GM a silent partner, He was invisible as well. It was none other than the Holy Spirit who gave Jesus discernment, directed His path and gave Him the power to do miracles.

"The Spirit of the Lord is on me, because he has anointed me to proclaim good news to the poor. He has sent me to proclaim freedom for the prisoners and recovery of sight for the blind, to set the oppressed free, to proclaim the year of the Lord's favor." (Luke 4:18-19/NIV)

When Jesus left the earth to return to God the Father in Heaven, He promised His disciples they would soon receive access to that same silent partner (Luke 24:49). The Holy Spirit would give them boldness and power to do miraculous things in God's name and would bring them comfort in the trying times to follow. As the disciples became known as apostles, the Holy Spirit worked behind the scenes to help them give birth to the Christian Church (Acts 2).

Anyone who has accepted Jesus as Savior and has been born again has access to that same silent partner. It certainly helps to have a spouse, a parent, a friend, a pastor, a business partner, etc., who can act as a general manager in our life, but the Holy Spirit will always be the perfect guide.

Here are a few ways you can take advantage of having a general manager in your life:

1. Seek someone out: Don't wait for someone to tell you they want to be your prayer warrior, your mentor or the head of your support system. Take a look around, find that person most likely to be willing to serve as a trustworthy silent partner in your life, and then ask them for prayer. Request their advice. Follow their example.

"Two people are better off than one, for they can help each other succeed." (Ecclesiastes 4:9/NIV)

2. Follow the Spirit: Even if you have an individual acting as your GM, know that you *still* need the workings of the Holy Spirit in your life at all times. People will fail you. They will unintentionally let you down. They may not have all the answers, but the Holy Spirit is perfectly able to guide your path and work behind the scenes on your behalf.

"For all who are led by the Spirit of God are children of God." (Romans 8:14/NIV)

3. Be someone else's general manager: Find someone else for whom you can be a silent partner. This might be your spouse, your child, a friend, or a co-worker. Pray for them. Be there when they need someone to talk to. Give them advice when they need direction. Seek the Holy Spirit on their behalf. Even as you need a GM in your life, don't miss out on the blessing of serving someone else in the same capacity.

"Therefore if you have any encouragement from being united with Christ, if any comfort from his love, if any common sharing in the Spirit, if any tenderness and compassion, then make my joy complete by being like-minded, having the same love, being one in spirit and of one mind." (Philippians 2:1-2/NIV)

No one can make it on his or her own. The most successful organizations or teams always have people like my wife Connie or Noah's wife who are quietly holding things together. Silent partners are never looking for the glory or the credit. In fact, they don't want it. They are doing it because they love you, and they want you to succeed.

Everybody needs a general manager.

Study Questions

1. What comes to mind when you think of the phrase "silent partner?" Who are some people that would identify as silent partners in your life, both past and present?

2. Can you think of a time when you didn't feel like you had much support in your endeavors? How did that impact your ability to be successful and what did you do to counter the lack of a silent partner?

3. Why is it so important to have moral, emotional and/or spiritual support during a difficult task (i.e. Coach Jarvis at St. John's, Noah and the ark, etc.)? Can you think of a situation where someone's prayers and encouragements got *you* through some challenging times?

4. What has been your experience with the Holy Spirit? Would you describe your relationship as A) non-existent B) a work in progress or C) totally engaged? If you answered A or B, what are some things that are keeping you from taking full advantage of the Holy Spirit's presence in your life?

5. Are you acting as the "general manager" or silent partner in someone else's life? If so, how has that been a blessing for both you and the other individual? If not, what is keeping you from taking on that role?

Prayer

Lord, thank You for the silent partners that You have placed in my path. I know that I cannot complete Your purposes without other individuals helping make things happen behind the scenes. Help me to recognize the Holy Spirit at work in my life. Help me do a better job following His lead. Allow me to be a blessing by taking on the role of silent partner in someone else's life. Amen.

CHAPTER EIGHT

THE ASSISTANT WHO SAVED MY LIFE
Everybody Needs Footsteps To Follow

"Leadership is not about titles, positions, or flowcharts. It is about one life influencing another." – John C. Maxwell

I graduated from Northeastern University in the spring of 1968. Later that year, I started teaching physical education at my alma mater, Rindge Technical High School. The following spring, I got a call from a lady at City Hall named Helen Hollum, a name I will never forgot. I had no idea why she wanted me to come see her, but she asked me to stop by her office for a visit within the next 24 to 48 hours.

Helen was a personable Irish Catholic lady who had some nice things to say and a very interesting piece of advice to share:

"I've been receiving great reports about your teaching," she said. "Headmaster Sweeney is really pleased with the job you are doing at the high school. We're so glad you came back to teach our kids in Cambridge. But you know, there's a war going on and we don't want to lose you."

Miss Hollum then told me that the only way I was going to be able to continue teaching and not be drafted was to start a family. Connie and I had six months to "get something going."

My wife Connie and I had planned on waiting five or six years to have children so we could save up enough money to buy a home. That night, I brought her some flowers and chocolates and broke the news.

"Honey, I think we're going to have to change our plans," I told her. "We need to start our family now."

At first, she thought I was kidding, but later that evening she agreed and we did as Miss Hollum suggested. Thanks to the good Lord, Connie was able to conceive, and on March 22, 1969, we had our first child, Michael Delaney Jarvis II, who would eventually earn the nickname Duece.

The Vietnam War was a long, costly, armed conflict that pitted North Vietnam's Communist regime and its allies, including Russia, against South Vietnam and its principal ally, the United States. This divisive war was increasingly unpopular at home and ended with the withdrawal of U.S. forces in 1973 and the unification of Vietnam under Communist control two years later. More than three million people, including 58,000 Americans were killed. Another 150,000 Americans were injured. If you weren't entitled, and especially if you were poor, you were likely going straight to the front lines.

Every one of my neighborhood friends who went to Vietnam, including my Little League teammate Gerald Phillips, either came back in a pine box or returned home as a drug addict or alcoholic. Not one person came back the same as they left.

My 12-Year Old Assistant

As soon as Mike could walk, the two of us were joined at the hip. In 1972, I was coaching the freshman high school baseball team on Hoyt Field, the same park where I grew up as a Little League player. Between 3:00 and 3:30 in the afternoon, my wife would pull up in our 1972 navy blue Volkswagen bug. The door would swing open, and my three-year old son would come running across the field. The first thing he would do was put on a batting helmet and then line up the bats. Mike was my batboy, and he took his job seriously.

Seven years later, at the age of 10, he assumed the position of ball boy at the high school and was at my side for all three of our championship photos. Monday through Friday, he would get out of school, board the bus on Massachusetts Avenue in North Cambridge and take the 10-minute ride to Harvard Square. He would then walk through the Harvard Yard and up Cambridge

Street all the way to the War Memorial Gymnasium where we practiced. Right around 4 p.m., Mike would run through the gym doors in the brown and gold sweat suit my wife had made for him. Two hours later, we would drive home together and catch up on what happened in school.

In 1981, my star player, Patrick Ewing, and I were invited to participate in the McDonald's All-American Game, the nation's top high school all-star exhibition. The organizers told me I could hand pick my assistant coach. I wanted to share this experience with Mike, so I chose him. When we arrived in Wichita, Kansas, and met the game's director at baggage claim, he wanted to know where my assistant was. Imagine the confused look on his face when I introduced him to Mike.

Mike took his role seriously and made the transition from ball boy to assistant with ease. Along with Patrick Ewing, the team included future stars such as Chris Mullin, Milt Wagner, Bill Wennington, Manuel Forest, Jeff Adkins, Adrian Branch, Buzz Peterson, Eugene McDowell and Michael Jordan. Back then there was no Internet or social media sites like Facebook and Twitter to feed the appetites of rabid college basketball fans. Because of that, I knew nothing about these players or how good they were. However, at the age of 12, Mike had a keen eye for talent and was immediately attracted to Michael Jordan's incredible skill and work ethic.

During our week together, Michael treated my son like he was his younger brother. Before the week was over, my Mike had a new hero. In fact, when we took the team picture, you could find the two MJ's standing side by side.

Mike's first game as an assistant took place on Easter Sunday in front of 18,000 fans and a national television audience. I think I was more nervous than him. I can't begin to tell you how proud I was when he was introduced and waived to the crowd. It was just two minutes into the game when Mike poked me in the side and made his first move as a coach.

"Dad, we've gotta get Adrian out of there," he earnestly advised. "He's not playing any defense. Let's get him out."

"You're right," I replied.

Now keep in mind, Adrian Branch was the number one high school player in the country. He played for the powerhouse DeMatha Catholic High School in Washington D.C., and would go on later that year to play at the University of Maryland. Adrian would eventually win an NBA Championship with the Los Angeles Lakers and spend several years playing professionally in Europe.

But on this night, my 12-year old assistant coach recognized that Adrian wasn't giving his best effort at the defensive end of the court. So I took him out of the game.

Adrian huffed over to the sideline, stormed past me and took a seat at the end of the bench. Mike got up, walked calmly to the end of the bench and knelt on one knee directly in front of Adrian. Then, Mike looked him in the eye and said:

"If you don't play defense, my dad's not gonna play you."

Mike stood up and returned to his seat next to me.

Adrian almost fell off his chair. He couldn't believe a 12-year old had called him out. About two more minutes ticked off the clock when Mike Jr. hit me with that elbow again.

"Dad, let's put Adrian back in," he said. "Let's give him another chance."

"Why not?" I responded.

When Adrian took the court, he played like a man possessed at both ends of the court. Our team played inspired basketball and won 96-95 on Michael Jordan's last-second basket. Adrian was named Most Valuable Player.

On that day, I knew my son was born to coach. Mike could evaluate talent, he had a great feel for the game, he loved to compete, and he wasn't afraid to make decisions. As we coached together over the years at George Washington University (where we became the first black father-son coaching duo in NCAA history), St. John's and Florida Atlantic University, I always conferred with Mike on my decisions, and 90 percent of the time we agreed.

One of the proudest moments of my coaching career occurred in 1993 when our George Washington Colonials received an at large bid to the NCAA tournament. In fact the last time GW made the tournament was 32 years earlier when John F. Kennedy had just been inaugurated as President of the United States. As a #12-seed, we traveled to Arizona, where we upset the #5 seed New Mexico. Two days later, we beat Southern University to earn a spot in the Sweet 16. With my son by my side, we traveled to Seattle and played an inspired game against the #1-ranked Michigan Wolverines. We gave the famed "Fab Five," a team that featured future NBA stars Jalen Rose, Juwan Howard and Chris Webber, all it could handle before losing 72-64.

People sometimes ask me, "What's the greatest thing that's ever happened to you as a coach?" or "What's the greatest award you've ever won?" I always tell them it was working side by side with Mike. Every morning when I woke up, whether it was a good day or a bad day, I knew that I was going to go to work with my son and my friend doing something we both love. That was the greatest award I could ever receive.

Mike had my back, and I had his. If he was down, I was up, and vice versa. I always respected the fact that Mike wasn't afraid to tell me the truth, whether I liked it or not. We made a great team. When we were together, I always felt like anything was possible.

Passing The Staff

Moses was arguably one of the greatest leaders to walk the face of the earth. He brought an entire nation out of slavery, communicated directly with God, and guided the Israelites to safety.

But Moses wasn't perfect. He made some significant mistakes along the way including one that cost him dearly. In Numbers 20:2-12, God instructed Moses to speak to a rock so it would pour out water for the complaining Israelites. In his frustration, Moses struck the rock with his staff instead. Water gushed from the rock, but because Moses disobeyed God's specific command and showed a lack of faith, he was not allowed to enter the Promised Land.

Prior to Moses' disobedience, he had been mentoring a young

man named Joshua. It's not likely that Moses was purposefully train-ing Joshua and preparing him for a future leadership role, but rather, the relationship was born out of necessity. Moses needed help, and he allowed Joshua to be a part of his daily routine. This led to some amazing opportunities for Joshua, including the chance to lead a group of spies into Canaan (Numbers 13:16) and a life-changing encounter with God. (Exodus 24:13-14)

Moses and Joshua's relationship was mutually beneficial. It was Moses' responsibility to pass the staff of leadership and prepare the next generation for the future. Joshua, on the other hand, was able to watch a seasoned leader in action. He gained valuable wisdom and knowledge from someone who had been tried and tested. Moses needed to leave footsteps that Joshua equally needed to fol-low.

As we later read in the Book of Joshua, Moses did his job well. The Israelites were in capable hands as their new leader guided them through many victorious battles and directed their path into Canaan.

The Boy That Would Be Kingmaker

Many years later, there was a woman named Hannah who wanted nothing more than to have a child. But the barren Jewish woman could not conceive, so she went to a man named Eli for prayer. Eli was a priest and one of the last Israelite judges. These men served as tribal leaders and served as military commanders dur-ing times of war. Eli blessed Hannah and assured her that she would have a child. (1 Samuel 1:19)

Sure enough, Hannah had a son. She was so elated that she promised she would give her child to God one day. She named her son Samuel, which means "The Name of God." When he was a young boy, Hannah brought him to Eli, who taught him the scrip-tures and trained him as if he were his own son. (1 Samuel 1:21-28)

One night, when Samuel was around the age of 12, he heard a voice calling his name in the middle of the night. Samuel thought it was Eli, so he went to the priest's room to see what he wanted.

"I did not call" Eli said. "Go back and lie down." (1 Samuel 3:6/NIV)

The same thing happened two more times that night. Eli finally realized it was God's voice calling to Samuel and told him to answer the voice the next time he heard it calling his name. The next time Samuel heard God's voice, he obediently responded:

"Speak, for your servant is listening." (1 Samuel 3:10/NIV)

The Lord then gave Samuel a prophetic word that included bad news for Eli and his family. God was going to pass judgment on Eli for overlooking his sons' blasphemous ways. Eli pressed Samuel for information about his vision. Samuel was reluctant but finally gave Eli the negative report. (1 Samuel 3:11-18)

Even still, Samuel spent the next several years with Eli, who trained the boy the ways of the priesthood. Eli had no way of knowing the great things Samuel would eventually do in that position. Samuel would go on to anoint the first two Kings of Israel, Saul and David. He would also become Israel's first recorded prophet and bridge the gap between two significant eras in that nation's history.

Without the time and effort that Eli put into Samuel's life, he may not have achieved the greatness to which God had called him. Eli's willingness to mentor Samuel may have seemed small at the time, but it had an immeasurable impact on Israel's future.

Everybody Needs Footsteps To Follow

Although the words "mentor" and "mentoring" are not specifically found in the Bible, there are many other great examples of the concept clearly demonstrated: Naomi and Ruth, Elisha and Elijah, Eli and Samuel, and Paul and Timothy, just to name a few.

Among the most studied and discussed, however, is the relationship between Jesus and His disciples. Throughout the Gospels, we see a loving, gentle father figure pouring into the lives of 12 men from a wide range of socio-economic backgrounds. He spent three years preparing them to fulfill their purpose as pioneers of the

Christian church. Most importantly, He modeled for them the greatest relationship of all time, the relationship between God the Father and His Son Jesus.

Just like Moses, Eli and Jesus, we are also called to pass the torch and prepare the next generation to take over. Here are three steps that can help us step out and fulfill that vital calling.

1. Find a mentor: We are never too old or so wise that we can no longer receive wisdom and instruction from others. Whether it's a parent, a grandparent, a friend, a pastor, a Christian business leader or coach, find someone who can speak into your life on a regular basis.

"As iron sharpens iron, so one person sharpens another." (Proverbs 27:17/NIV)

2. Cultivate the relationship with your children: For those parents reading this book, make a conscious effort to be a mentor in their lives. If you have already started this process, continue doing so and find ways to be more effective in your training and parental leadership.

"Train up a child in the way he should go, and when he is old he will not depart from it." (Proverbs 22:6/NKJV)

3. Find others to mentor: You might not be a parent, or perhaps your children are grown. That doesn't mean you can't be a mentor. Find a young person who doesn't have a parent or perhaps someone who just needs extra guidance in their life. Get involved with a youth ministry, a sports team, a civic youth organization or a community school program. It won't take long to discover someone seeking leadership and guidance. Be intentional with your time, talent and experience. Share it!

"Be shepherds of God's flock that is under your care, watching over them—not because you must, but because you are willing, as God wants you to be; not pursuing dishonest gain, but eager to serve." (1 Peter 5:2/NIV)

God has built us to leave a legacy. We need someone to follow our footsteps. It's amazing how God blesses us in our service to others.

When my son was born, he shielded me from the throes of a brutal war. Mike literally saved my life. But it went further than that. His presence gave me the opportunity to become a mentor and helped me to be the dad I never had. Mentoring Mike has been a blessing for both me and my wife. I can't begin to tell you how proud we are of him as we observe his interactions with his family, friends and others.

Mentoring does more for you than it does for your children. Even if you don't have children or your children are now grown, you can still mentor others and continue fulfilling your obligation and your purpose.

"Let your light so shine before men, that they may see your good works and glorify your Father which is in Heaven." (Matthew 5:16/KJV)

Everybody needs footsteps to follow.

Study Questions

1. Who was someone that you looked up to when you were a child or a young person? How did that individual positively impact and influence your life?

2. Do you have children? If so, how have you purposefully mentored and trained them?

3. Thinking about the stories referenced (Coach Jarvis and his son, Moses and Joshua, Eli and Samuel and Jesus and the disciples), what is the significance of leaving footsteps for others to follow? What are the benefits for the mentor? What are the benefits for the one *being* mentored?

4. Do you currently have a mentor in your life? If so, how has the person helped you? If not, what is keeping you from finding a mentor?

5. Are you actively involved in mentoring someone other than one of your own children? If so, how has that relationship been mutually beneficial? If not, what is keeping you from finding someone else to mentor?

6. What are some things you can do now that will help you become more open to or more involved in the mentoring concept? What are some ways that you expect the process to change your life and the lives of those within your circle of influence?

Prayer

Lord, thank You for the people that You have placed in my life as mentors. I would not be where I am today if not for their wisdom and guidance. Just as You have put these people in my path, allow me to encounter others that need my compassionate leadership and direction. I want to leave a legacy that makes a difference and brings You glory. Amen.

CHAPTER NINE

THE EDUCATION OF PATRICK EWING
Everybody Needs An Investment

"Mentoring is not only an investment in the life of one child but also an investment in the future of our nation. A mentor demonstrates vision, shows unconditional care while providing life-changing affirmation."
– *Tom Osborne*

When we think of the word "investment," it's usually the financial connotations that first come to mind. After all, monetary investment is the fuel that keeps the the free market's economic engine turning.

But money isn't the only thing we can invest. In fact, it's really not even the most important thing. Instead, it is other valuable resources like time, emotional support, wisdom, friendship, kindness and love that often make the biggest differences in our world. And just like a financial investment, these relational investments always yield a good return, especially when we're talking about the Kingdom of God.

Sometimes it's easy to forget that the investments you are making today, into the lives of your children, your friends, your neighbors, your students, your athletes, etc., will bring back a return someday. From my personal experience, I know very well just how rewarding relational investments can be, even if they weren't obvious at the time.

The Next Bill Russell

In 1975, I was working as a physical education teacher at what was then called Rindge Technical High School in Cambridge, Massachusetts. I was also serving as an assistant men's basketball coach at Harvard University.

One day, my good friend Steve Jenkins approached me with an unusual request. He was the P.E. teacher at Achievement School, an alternative junior high program, which was housed in our building. Achievement School was designed to teach junior high students who were having difficulties, as well as foreign students that were transitioning into the American culture.

I had just finished teaching one of my morning P.E. classes when Steve introduced me to a seventh grader named Patrick Ewing. He had just moved from Jamaica to Cambridge. Patrick was about 6-3 and very thin. He was also very shy and had a heavy Jamaican accent.

Steve was a football coach and didn't know as much about basketball. He wanted me to teach Patrick how to play basketball. Patrick played soccer and cricket when he was younger, but he had literally outgrown those sports.

"Why do you want Patrick to play basketball?" I asked Steve. "Is it because he's tall?"

"Yeah, he's tall," Steve replied. "It's probably the best sport for him. But the main reason is because I want him to make friends. I want him to meet other kids and develop some meaningful relationships."

So I started working with Patrick on the fundamentals of basketball, such as dribbling, passing and shooting. We also worked on his overall body strength and footwork with a daily dose of pushups, sit-ups and jump rope. Every practice began with the Mikan Drill, named after Lakers Hall of Fame Center George Mikan, one of basketball's original big men. This helped Patrick develop his right-handed and left-handed hook shots. We ended each session with free throws.

Patrick's most impressive character traits were his focus, his concentration and his work ethic. I can't remember him ever saying something was too hard or that he couldn't do it. He always tried his best.

During his junior high school days, Patrick started to make friends around school and in the community, but there were some kids who called him names. They made fun of his slight frame and his Jamaican accent. When he played pickup games on the courts behind his house or at the nearby indoor facility, called "The Mission," some of the older players tried to push him around in an attempt to break his spirit. The more they tried to discourage and intimidate him, though, the harder he pushed back and the more determined he became.

When Patrick played, his main concern was helping his team. It was always about winning. He never complained when his teammates didn't pass him the ball, and he always hustled. Patrick ran from one end of the court to the other as fast as he could for as long as he could.

One night, I was at his house watching a basketball game with him in his living room. Legendary NBA center Moses Malone was playing for the Houston Rockets.

"Doc, doc!" Patrick spoke up. "Moses ain't runnin'! He ain't runnin' the floor! What's up with that?"

"That's how most centers in the NBA play," I explained," But you run and play defense like Bill Russell, the greatest center of all time. Keep playing the way you play, and you can be the next Bill Russell."

Years later, Patrick told me that back then he didn't know who Bill Russell was, but because winning was his main concern (just like Russell), I didn't have to motivate him to give his all. That was another one of his character traits. Patrick had no sense of limitation. His ability to play defense, rebound and block shots earned the respect of his teammates, gave him great personal gratification, and fueled his passion for the game.

While I was working privately with Patrick during the day and coaching at Harvard at night, I had no idea that four years later I would be his high school coach. Our first year together as player and coach was Patrick's sophomore year. He was 6-9 and weighed 165 pounds. By the time he was a senior, he was 7-feet tall, weighed 235 pounds and had developed into the most dominant high school basketball player in America. Together, we recorded an almost perfect record of 77-1 and became the #1-ranked team in the nation. Every game we played, including the contests we played at the Boston Garden, was sold out. Everyone wanted to beat Patrick and the Mighty Warriors!

From the mid-1970s until the mid-1980s, the city of Boston was enacting forced busing policies in an effort to integrate the schools. Amid the heightened racial tensions, our games took on a life of their own. On two separate occasions, the tires on our bus were slashed and bricks were thrown through the windows. The name-calling and chants from the crowd became more and more personal. "Ewing can't read!" was one of the more popular taunts used to rattle our star player. In one particularly distasteful moment during the state tournament, an opposing fan dressed up in a gorilla suit. What I didn't know at the time was that Patrick got through all of this because of the support and faith of his mother and family.

Although I wasn't aware of it at the time, I now realize the nine years I spent working as a college assistant at Northeastern and Harvard were God's way of preparing me to coach the #1 player in the country. My college experience also helped me better handle the intense college recruiting that would follow. There is no way I would have been able to deal with everything had I been a young novice coach.

Thanks to the faith that Mrs. Ewing had in me, we were able to do everything the right way and put Patrick in a position to make a great college choice. In the end, he chose to play for John Thompson and Georgetown University over a litany of legendary coaches including Rick Pitino (Boston University), Dr. Tom Davis (Boston College), Rollie Massimino (Villanova), Larry Brown (UCLA) and Dean Smith (North Carolina).

When Patrick went to Georgetown, he was ready to compete and win at the highest level. He was a three-time All-American, played in three national championship games, was the 1984 National Player of the Year, and the key player on the Hoyas' 1984 NCAA Championship team.

A few months after Patrick graduated from Georgetown in 1985, he became the first NBA Lottery draft selection when the New York Knicks selected him with their #1 pick. Patrick spent 17 years in the NBA, mostly with the New York Knicks, where he was 1986 Rookie of the Year and an 11-time All-Star. After becoming a naturalized U.S. citizen during his college days, he also won an Olympic gold medal in 1984 and repeated the feat in 1992 on the Dream Team alongside Michael Jordan, Magic Johnson, Larry Bird, Charles Barkley, Chris Mullin, David Robinson, Karl Malone, Scottie Pippen, John Stockton, Clyde Drexler and Christian Lattner. In 2008, I was in attendance when Patrick received the ultimate honor and was inducted into the Naismith Basketball Hall of Fame in Springfield, Massachussetts.

Since retiring as a player, Patrick has become a highly successful NBA assistant coach and become known for developing post players like Dwight Howard. But Patrick is much more than that. He's a winner, and he knows what it takes to be a champion. He also has a high basketball I.Q. Most importantly, Patrick is a man of character. When he gets his opportunity to be an NBA head coach, I will know that the time I invested into his life was better spent than I could have ever imagined.

The Woman Behind The Big Man

After Patrick's gold medal performance at the 1984 Olympics, the City of Cambridge honored its native son with a parade that started at City Hall and ended at Cambridge Rindge and Latin High School. Patrick was given the opportunity to speak to the high school student body, many of his former teachers, and his adoring fans. The mayor officially proclaimed it to be "Patrick Ewing Day." I was given the honor of introducing my prized pupil.

As I talked about Patrick, all I could think about was his mother Dorothy and how she made it possible for her son to come into this world, move to the greatest country on Earth, and develop into the player and person that we were there to honor. There would be no

"Patrick Ewing Day" if it weren't for Dorothy Ewing and the valuable lessons she taught him. I gave 10 examples of how those lessons were exemplified in Patrick's life:

1. Patrick had perfect attendance. He never missed a practice, game or class.
2. He always sat in the front row. Patrick didn't want to miss a thing.
3. Patrick listened with his eyes and ears. He perfected the art of listening.
4. He was not afraid to ask questions. Patrick would raise his hand and keeping asking questions until he understood. Once he had it, he never forgot it.
5. Patrick was not afraid to fail.
6. He did the little things.
7. He played to win.
8. He never made excuses.
9. He selected his friends wisely.
10. Patrick gave thanks. He always thanked his family, his teammates, his coaches, his friends, his teachers, and God.

At the end of my speech, I told everyone how blessed I was to have had the opportunity to coach Patrick. Unfortunately, Dorothy wasn't in attendance that day. She had passed away during Patrick's sophomore year at Georgetown. I did, however, share with the audience that his mother was looking down on her boy from Heaven with joy in her heart and a big smile on her face.

Yes, I invested in Patrick's life, but Dorothy was the person who deserved most of the credit. Most of the people in the crowd that day weren't fully aware of how much she had poured into him. She was a strong Christian woman who ran her home with a firm but loving hand.

Dorothy wanted the best for her children and their future, so she decided that she and her husband Carl would move to the United States and prepare a way for her children. The Ewings settled in

Cambridge, where Dorothy took a job in the food service depart-
ment at Massachusetts General Hospital. Together, Dorothy and
Carl saved enough money to send for their five daughters and two
sons, one at a time.

The nine members of the Ewing family lived in a five-room
apartment down the road from me on River Street. In that close-knit
environment, Patrick learned the true meaning of commitment, hard
work, determination and sacrifice from his mother. As he was growing up, she encouraged him to play sports, to never give up, to be
true to his word, and to finish what he started. Years later, Patrick
decided against an early entry into the NBA and elected to stayed in
college instead. He had promised his mother that he would earn a
college degree and there was no way he was going back on that
promise.

I was once asked what was Dorothy Ewing's cause of death. My
response: "Hard work." I know that if she were alive today, she
would say that all of the time and love she gave Patrick was more
than worth it. Dorothy would be proud to see the incredible return
on her priceless investment.

The Woman Behind The Savior

In 1865, William Ross Wallace published a poem that made this
famous declaration: "The hand that rocks the cradle is the hand that
rules the world."

It's hard to argue with Wallace's assertion about the powerful
influence mothers have wielded from the beginning of time, but
there is only *one* mother who can be given credit for playing a part
in actually *saving* the world. Her name was Mary and she was a
young woman from Nazareth. She was engaged to a man named
Joseph, who was a descendent of David.

Mary's life changed forever, however, when the angel Gabriel
appeared to her and brought some unexpected news.

"You will conceive and give birth to a son, and you are to call
him Jesus. He will be great and will be called the Son of the Most

High. The Lord God will give him the throne of his father David, and he will reign over Jacob's descendents forever; his kingdom will never end." (Luke 1:31-33/NIV)

Gabriel's message was stunning for a number of reasons. First of all, Mary was a virgin. When asked how it would be possible for her to have a child, the angel explained that the Holy Spirit would miraculously make it so. Mary would also have to tell Joseph that she was pregnant and trust that God would reveal the truth about her divine selection.

Then there was the revelation that this wouldn't just be any child. This would be the Son of God! And just as astonishing was the prophecy that He would one day become the King of Kings. Mary must have been filled with joy and fear at the same time, yet her response showed why God was able to entrust her with such a great responsibility.

"I am the Lord's servant," Mary answered. "May your word be fulfilled." (Luke 1:38/NIV)

Can you imagine how Mary must have felt as she raised Jesus? Here she was, an ordinary Jewish woman doing her best to invest all of her time and love into a child who would one day alter the course of history. At the time, Mary had no idea exactly what that meant. She didn't know that her son would become the ultimate sacrifice for mankind's sins. Mary only knew what Gabriel had told her. She understood it was her job to support Jesus in His journey to become the destined Savior of the world.

Mary must have been filled with joy as she watched Jesus enter into His ministry. Surely she was humbled to know that she had successfully completed her part of God's mission, but she also must have been heartbroken to see her falsely-accused son being whipped, beaten, bruised, mocked, tormented and crucified on the Cross.

Mary didn't know it yet, but Jesus' death wasn't the end of the story. Three days after He was buried, His tomb was found to be empty. Shortly thereafter, Jesus appeared to several of His followers. When Mary saw her resurrected son, I can imagine that she finally grasped the true value of the years she had spent investing in His life. As she listened to Jesus share with His disciples what was to come, surely Mary realized that her part in all of this was going to continue to make an impact for generations to come and indeed, for all of eternity.

Everybody Needs An Investment

As important as it is to make wise financial investments, it's even more important to make wise relational investments. The Bible talks often about money and how we should be good stewards of our resources, but even more so, the scriptures tell us that the greatest investments we can make are into the lives of those around us.

Sometimes we think we need a lot of money to help people, but money and material resources are only a small part of the equation when it comes to relational investment. Here are three simple ways we can make deposits on a daily basis:

1. Invest resources: It doesn't matter what our economic status may be, we all have things we can physically give to those in need. Perhaps it's a used pair of basketball shoes that can be donated to an aspiring athlete in the neighborhood who can't afford his or her own. Maybe it's a bag of groceries for a widowed lady who is having trouble making ends meet or maybe it's clothes to the homeless. There are limitless ways we can invest in the wellbeing of others.

"In everything I did, I showed you that by this kind of hard work we must help the weak, remembering the words the Lord Jesus himself said: 'It is more blessed to give than to receive.'" (Acts 20:35/NIV)

2. Invest kindness: Relational investments don't have to cost a penny. We can be kind to people we know and lift their spirits. We can be kind to total strangers and make their day. A thoughtful word or gesture might be the one thing that helps someone else get through a difficult moment in his or her life.

"Be kind and compassionate to one another, forgiving each other, just as in Christ God forgave you." (Ephesians 4:32/NIV)

3. Invest wisdom: Find a young person, maybe a child, a teenager or a young adult, who needs direction. This doesn't necessarily have to be your own child, but that doesn't mean you can't impart knowledge and wisdom into their hearts. And just like with your kids, those shared experiences will leave an indelible mark.

"Start children off on the way they should go, and even when they are old they will not turn from it." (Proverbs 22:6/NIV)

4. Invest time: Sometimes the simplest way we can invest in others is to just be there for them. Hugs and smiles are priceless. Ears that listen and shoulders that are available to be cried on have immeasurable value. Showing you care is often as easy as being available.

"Rejoice with those who rejoice; mourn with those who mourn." (Romans 12:15/NIV)

Farmers reap the harvest that comes from planting and watering seeds. Financiers reap a monetary gain on capital investments. And all of us, as ordinary, everyday people, can get back the incredible reward of seeing how our resources, our kindness, our wisdom and our time can change someone else's life. You never know what great things those recipients might accomplish one day.

Everybody needs an investment.

Study Questions

1. Have you ever invested money or resources into a business venture? If so, what were your expectations and your hopes for what might come from that investment?

2. Can you think of someone who has invested into your life? Explain what that looked like and how it impacted the person you are today.

3. Have you ever invested in someone else's life? If so, what was the result of that investment?

4. Of the four types of relational investment listed, which ones are easiest for you to contribute? Explain.

5. Which of those relational investments is more difficult for you to give up? Explain.

6. What are some things you can start doing today that will allow you to invest in other people's lives on a more regular basis? What are your expectations and your hopes for what might come from those investments?

Prayer

Lord, thank You for putting people in my life who have invested in me with their resources, their kindness, their wisdom and their time. Give me a stronger desire to invest in others. Bless me with greater resources that I can pass along. Grant me wisdom that I can share. Help me be a better steward of my time so that I might encourage others to fulfill the purpose to which You have called them. Amen.

CHAPTER TEN

A TIME TO FIGHT
Everybody Needs To
Stand For Something

"Silence in the face of evil is itself evil: God will not hold us guiltless. Not to speak is to speak. Not to act is to act." – Dietrich Bonhoeffer

Strive for peace, but stand up and fight when necessary.

That was the message I learned from leaders like Martin Luther King Jr., Robert F. Kennedy, and Red Auerbach. MLK was a social activist. RFK was a politician. Auerbach was a coach. All three men were trying to usher in a new era of racial equality.

Red, for instance, wanted to have the best team he could possibly have and the color of a player's skin didn't matter. I'll never forget that night on December 26, 1964 as I listened to a radio broadcast of the Celtics game. Red made history when he became the first coach to start five black players in an NBA game.

A week later, my brother Richard and I were in the Boston Garden to see it with our own eyes. It was a defining moment for the game of basketball, the NBA, and the racially divided city of Boston. It had a profound and lasting effect on me as a fan, a player, and an aspiring coach. Red's courage inspired me and gave me hope.

Unfortunately, those who tried to bring white and black people together back then were putting themselves in a dangerous position. MLK knew it was just a matter of time before he would be assassinated. The same was tragically true for RFK. Fortunately, Red was able to escape any real threats to his life, but he certainly dealt with his share of criticism for breaking through the color barrier.

They stood up. They stood out. They fought for justice. They made our world a better place.

Standing Up

As my coaching career progressed, I was blessed to reap the benefits that came from the seeds those men and many others treacherously sowed. But that didn't mean my journey was completely free of obstacles, challenges, and even some injustices along the way.

After nine years of waiting (and nearly giving up on my dream job), I was finally offered the chance to coach the varsity boy's basketball team at Cambridge Rindge and Latin High School. The Cambridge community expected a state championship, and we gave them what they wanted. We went undefeated in 27 games and were ranked among the top 10 teams in the nation.

My star player, Patrick Ewing, was considered by many to be the #1 center prospect in high school. Every major college basketball program wanted Patrick, but when the coaches came to see him, they often discovered our other talented players. Because of that, many players in search of a college scholarship wanted to play with Patrick and the mighty Warriors of CRLS. On several occasions, players from outside the city and even outside the state approached us about transferring to Cambridge. There was one catch. Because we were a public school, students had to be a legal resident of the city in order to play on our team.

This was the case with a phenomenal point guard from Boston named Karl Hobbs. In the summer of 1979, Karl's mother moved to Florida, but he decided to stay in the Boston area. He wanted to make a better way for himself. Karl was 18, a legal adult, and took up residence with the Murrell family in Cambridge. It was completely permissible, but Joe Day, Karl's head coach at Jeremiah E. Burke High School, was upset that he had lost his star player. Coach Day accused me of recruiting Karl and took his case to the Massachusetts Intercollegiate Athletic Association (MIAA).

The truth of that matter is this: I didn't recruit Karl Hobbs. He recruited me. Karl wanted to earn a Division I scholarship and knew his best chance was in my basketball program. He also knew there was a possibility that the MIAA could rule him ineligible for the entire year, but he was willing to take the chance. Karl was cleared to play just before Christmas, but that wasn't the end of the battle.

Throughout the season, I did my best to shield the players from the legal battle taking place between the MIAA and our program. It wasn't easy, but we stayed focused on coaching the kids and putting them in the best position to succeed. There were some close calls, but we usually found a way to win. During the regular season, we lost one non-league game to the Connecticut State Champs, Wilbur Cross High School.

One week before the start of the state playoffs, the MIAA reversed its decision and declared Karl ineligible. On top of that, they said our team would be disqualified as well. The city of Cambridge took the MIAA to court and filed an injunction to allow our team to play. The judge ruled in our favor and we went on to win our second of three consecutive Division I state championships.

I didn't realize how difficult the battle was until it was over. It was bigger than just winning basketball games; I was fighting for my coaching life and my reputation. More importantly, I was fighting for my players and their futures. They had been caught in the cross-fire. For the majority of them, I was their substitute dad and their symbol of hope. I was their link between the present and a brighter future.

All but two of the players from those CRLS teams went on to attend institutions of higher learning. One became a fireman. The other became a policeman in Cambridge.

Patrick Ewing went on to play at Georgetown and eventually in the NBA, where he had a Hall of Fame career as one of the greatest centers to ever play the game. Karl Hobbs earned a scholarship to the University of Connecticut and had an outstanding career playing for Don Perno and legendary head coach Jim Calhoun. After his brief pro career, I hired Karl as an assistant at Boston University. After that, he worked as an assistant at Connecticut before moving on to become the head coach at George Washington University. After 10 years there, Karl rejoined the Connecticut coaching staff as an assistant to Kevin Ollie and helped them win the 2014 NCAA Championship.

It was much more than Patrick and Karl's success that made it all worthwhile. It was my way of repaying all of the people who had given me the courage to stand up and fight for what I believed in.

Eleven years after winning the battle against the MIAA, I was inducted into the Massachusetts Basketball Coaches Association Hall of Fame in front of my family and a host of friends from Cambridge.

The Original Freedom Fighter

From the beginning of time, people who have stood up against injustice have also stood out in the public square and drawn the attention of those in authority. Sometimes standing out is a good thing, but in too many instances, it puts a proverbial bull's eye on the messenger and leads to uncomfortable scrutiny.

One prominent Old Testament hero found this out on two separate occasions, each of which produced much different results. His name was Moses, and he was a Hebrew born during a time of Egyptian slavery. The king, commonly referred to as Pharaoh, had called for the oppression of God's people. He was fearful of their growing population. (Exodus 1:8-14)

As the Israelites grew in number, Pharaoh took even more extreme measures and ordered that all newborn Israelite boys be drowned in the Nile River. Moses' mother Jochebed wanted desperately to save her son, so she placed him in a basket and concealed it in the tall reeds near the riverbank. Pharaoh's daughter discovered the basket and decided to adopt Moses as her own. She even enlisted Jochebed's help thanks to Moses' older sister Miriam who had secretly been watching from a distance. (Exodus 2:1-10)

Moses seemed to be destined for greatness. Why else would his life be miraculously spared? Yet Moses didn't appear to understand this during his young adult years. He was raised as royalty and lived a life of luxury. One day, however, Moses became curious about the

Hebrews. He wanted to know more about his people. So he went out to the fields of labor and watched as the Egyptian taskmasters cruelly and relentlessly ruled over the helpless slaves. One scene in particular caught his attention.

"He saw an Egyptian beating a Hebrew, one of his own people. Looking this way and that and seeing no one, he killed the Egyptian and hid him in the sand." (Exodus 2:11-12/NIV)

The next day, Moses realized that his moment of murderous rage was no longer a secret. His attempt at seeking justice for the Hebrew slave backfired, and he was forced to flee Egypt before Pharaoh could track him down. Moses settled in Midian where he took a wife and started a family.

Many years later, Moses had an opportunity for redemption. God famously spoke to him through a burning bush and sent him back to Egypt to bring the Israelites out of slavery. At first, Moses was afraid. He was just a lowly shepherd and, to make matters worse, a man with a criminal past. But God gave Moses some specific instructions and promised that He would raise His mighty hand against the Egyptian oppressors. (Exodus 3-4)

By this time, a new Pharaoh had taken rule over Egypt. Moses went back to the Hebrew people there and reconnected with his older brother Aaron. As God had commanded, they approached Pharaoh and requested that their people be allowed to leave for three days in order to go through the ritual of animal sacrifice. After Pharaoh denied the request, God then brought the infamous 10 plagues against the Egyptian people, which ultimately caused Pharaoh to tell Moses and the Hebrews to leave. That led to the showdown at the Red Sea where God parted the waters and allowed the Israelites to cross safely to the other side. When Pharaoh and his army tried to follow them, God caused the waters to crash down and wipe them out. (Exodus 5-14)

As a young man, Moses fought injustice the wrong way. He allowed pride and anger to get the best of him. Moses took matters into his own hand. It was an ineffective short-term solution to a long-term problem. Had Moses kept his cool and remained in the palace, perhaps he would have grown in power and authority and brought justice to his people in another way. Instead, decades passed before deliverance came to the Israelites.

When Moses returned, he had positioned himself to be an effective freedom fighter. He was a humbled leader who understood his limitations and was fully dependent on his Creator. This time, it was God's plan, in God's timing and with God's help. Injustice didn't have a chance, and in the process, God performed one of the greatest miracles known to man.

A New Kind of Justice

When Jesus arrived on the scene over 2,000 years ago, He brought with Him a message that turned the concept of justice on its head. The Jewish people anticipated the arrival of a Messiah who would overthrow the heavy-handed Roman Empire and reign over an earthly kingdom. While many were intrigued with Jesus' teachings about peace, hope and love, others were disappointed to find out that He wasn't planning a government takeover.

Instead, Jesus displayed a new kind of justice through several powerful encounters with everyday people.

Jesus rejected racism: He treated people from different races and nationalities the same. Although He naturally spent a great deal of time amongst the Jews, Jesus never shied away from sharing the Gospel with Gentiles like the Samaritan woman He met at the well (John 4:1-42). Additionally, it was a Samaritan who played the role of compassionate hero in Jesus' parable about kindness and good will (Luke 10:25-37). These instances were in spite of the fact that Jews generally considered Samaritans to be second-class citizens.

Jesus rejected classism: He dealt with the poor in the same way He dealt with the rich. They were equal in His eyes. Jesus also commanded His followers to take care of the poor (Luke 14:12-14) and publicly commended a widow for putting her last two mites into the temple treasury (Luke 21:1-4).

Jesus rejected sexism: He never talked down to women in a culture where women were often considered voiceless and powerless. In fact, he honored women such as Mary and Martha (Luke 10:38-42) and the woman who was healed when she touched the hem of His garment. (Luke 8:43-48)

Jesus rejected totalitarianism: He could have come to Earth and set up an omnipotent kingdom. But instead, Jesus showed His disciples a different way to rule that defied human logic. After an argument amongst His closest followers about which ones would reign in God's Heavenly kingdom, Jesus introduced them to the concept of servant leadership:

"You know that the rulers of the Gentiles lord it over them, and their high officials exercise authority over them. Not so with you. Instead, whoever wants to become great among you must be your servant, and whoever wants to be first must be your slave–just as the Son of Man did not come to be served, but to serve, and to give His life as a ransom for many." (Matthew 20:25-28/NIV)

Jesus rejected prejudice: Besides the divide between races, nationalities, genders and classes, there were many other groups that were oppressed, looked down upon, or flat out ignored. Jesus didn't just preach against this type of prejudice, he demonstrated what it looks like to tear down walls that separate people. He allowed a woman known for her sinful life to wash His feet with her expensive perfume (Luke 7:36-50). He shared a meal with Zacchaeus, a corrupt tax collector (Luke 19:1-10). He stopped an adulterous woman from being stoned to death (John 8:1-11). He healed 10 lepers who had been exiled from the community (Luke 17:11-19). In each of those stories, Jesus' rejection of prejudice forever changed the people He encountered.

Jesus stood out as he went against societal norms and included people in His group of followers who would usually be excluded: the lowly, the despised, the disenfranchised, the poor, the sinner, and the unimportant. He also showed no preference toward the Jew or the Gentile and rankled religious leaders in the process.

That's what happens when you bring people together; It makes them uncomfortable. As history has shown us, that's when prominent leaders are attacked, sometimes to the point of assassination or execution.

God knew how the people would respond to Jesus' message. He knew that pride and fear would hinder the masses from accepting the true application of justice. Because Jesus now presented a threat to the status quo, He was given over to the Roman authorities and crucified for a crime that He did not commit.

Everybody Needs To Stand For Something

Sometimes it's easy to look at leaders like Martin Luther King, Robert F. Kennedy, Dietrich Bonhoeffer and Moses, and feel unable to step into such big shoes. It's an especially daunting task when you look at the way Jesus dealt with the societal wrongs of His time. It may not seem like we all have that kind of influence, but every voice matters.

As Bonhoeffer said, "Silence in the face of evil is itself evil." In other words, we are all called to stand against injustice, and more importantly, stand *for* justice. This is our moral obligation as a society and as followers of Christ. Standing up for justice is first and foremost our obligation and not doing so can bring grave consequences.

The prophet Isaiah gave this warning to the Kingdom of Judah during 8th Century BC:

"Woe to those who make unjust laws, to those who issue oppressive decrees, to deprive the poor of their rights and withhold justice from the oppressed of my people, making widows their prey and robbing the fatherless." (Isaiah 10:1-2/NIV)

And King Solomon shared this nugget of divine wisdom that rings true today:

"Whoever oppresses the poor shows contempt for their Maker, but whoever is kind to the needy honors God." (Proverbs 14:31/NIV)

Jesus further expounded on these teachings when He encouraged His followers to give food to the hungry, give drink to the thirsty, give clothes to the unclothed, take care of the sick, and visit the prisoner.

"Truly, I tell you, whatever you did for one of the least of these brothers and sisters of mine, you did for Me." (Matthew 25:20/NIV)

Unfortunately, we have all too often abdicated that responsibility to the various levels of governments, and sometimes, we look at the private organizations doing humanitarian work and assume their efforts are good enough. Other times, it's simply a matter of being too busy with our own lives to get involved. That mentality must come to an end if we are to truly see an end to injustice in this world and show people what God's love is all about.

Here are a few ways we can reclaim the calling that has been given to each of us, to fight for justice in an unjust world:

1. Look Up (For Divine Perspective): Make a conscious effort to look at people through God's eyes. See others as He sees them, and as He sees you, as valued and divinely loved creations.

"So God created mankind in his own image, in the image of God he created them; male and female he created them." (Genesis 1:27/NIV)

2. Speak Up (For The Voiceless): If you see someone being teased, bullied, cheated, oppressed or mistreated, say something about it. Step in and make your voice heard. Don't let fear or pride allow you to stand by idly as a family member, friend, co-worker or total stranger is treated unjustly.

"Speak out on behalf of the voiceless, and for the rights of all who are vulnerable. Speak out in order to judge with righteousness and to defend the needy and the poor." Proverbs 31:8-9 (CEB)

3. Team Up (For The Better): Find people who also want to fight injustice and work together. Moses needed Aaron. I needed support from my family, friends and legal counsel. No one should go it alone. We are better and more effective when we work together.

"Two are better than one, because they have a good return for their labor." (Ecclesiastes 4:9/NIV)

4. Stand Up (For The Cause): Get involved with efforts to fight injustice through the support and active involvement with organizations that feed and clothe the impoverished, work to end slavery, defend the rights of women and children, protect all stages of life, care for orphans, and assist those who have faced great tragedy. Words don't mean much until they become action.

"This is what the Lord says: Do what is just and right. Rescue from the hand of the oppressor the one who has been robbed. Do no wrong or violence to the foreigner, the fatherless or the widow, and do not shed innocent blood in this place." (Jeremiah 22:3/NIV)

Most importantly, make sure whatever causes you support line up with the biblical concept of justice and that everything you do is an expression of God's love. It's impossible to go wrong when His Word and the life of Christ is your standard for administering mercy and grace to those who need it the most.

"He is the Rock, His works are perfect, and all His ways are just. A faithful God who does no wrong, upright and just is He." (Deuteronomy 32:4/NIV)

Everybody needs to stand for something.

Study Questions

1. What is the first thing that comes to mind when you hear the word "justice?" What about the word "injustice?"

2. Have you ever dealt with a situation where you felt like you were being treated unjustly? How did you respond, and how was the situation resolved?

3. Who are some people you have observed that you would say have stood against injustice, in your community or on a larger scale? What are some of those people's qualities that you admire and/or wish you also had?

4. Thinking back to Moses' story, what are some problems that can take place when you take justice into your own hands? What did Moses do right the second time he fought against injustice and why do you think those actions produced more favorable results?

5. Of the injustices listed Jesus rejected, which ones have you felt most strongly about and worked the hardest against? Which of the injustices listed have you paid the least attention to or haven't thought as much about fighting against?

6. Do you actively support any causes that fight injustice? If so, what are they? If not, what's keeping you from doing so and what can you start doing today to get more involved?

Prayer

Lord, help me see people the way You see them. Help me identify any unjust activities taking place around me. Give me the courage to stand up for the oppressed and to be a voice for the voiceless. Teach me the biblical meaning of justice so that I might apply it to my life and help others find justice in their lives. Amen.

CHAPTER ELEVEN

CLOSED DOORS, OPEN WINDOWS
Everybody Needs
A Game Changing Moment

"Change is the law of life. And those who look only to the past or present are certain to miss the future." – John F. Kennedy

One moment. That's all it takes. One moment can change everything. One moment can determine the course of a life. Sometimes there's no choice but to be altered after such an event. Other times, these defining moments can create an incredibly important decision for the future.

I like to call it a game changing moment.

We don't always enjoy change. In fact, often times, we resist it. Stepping out of our comfort zone and doing something different can present unwanted challenges. That's why game changing moments are so crucial and necessary. They have the power to move us forward and bring us closer to our destiny.

One Swing

September 13, 1981 is a day that will always be special to the Jarvis family. Just six months earlier, I had coached the Cambridge boy's high school basketball team to its third consecutive Division 1 state championship. Still basking in the glow of that moment, I sat in the bleachers at the North Cambridge little league baseball field with my wife Connie and my daughter Dana. We were there to watch my 12-year old son Mike play in the season-ending city championship.

Mike had finally grown out of the uniform that his mom had

sewed together for him. We sat there and reminisced about the first game he wore that #2 jersey. Mike was a very talented athlete. Baseball was the sport we thought might give him the best chance to play in college. He could field. He could hit. He could throw.

In this particular game, Mike was the pitcher. He was having a great game on the mound, but he was also showing off his skills at the plate. The municipal swimming pool was right behind the outfield fence. Every time Mike came up to bat, my wife would yell, "Pool it! Pool it!" In other words, she wanted him to hit it out of the ballpark and into the pool.

In the last inning, Mike came up to bat with his team trailing and runners on base. He was just trying to get a hit, but instead he hit a monstrous home run. Mike hit the ball so hard that it not only flew over the fence, but over the pool as well. Mike had the biggest smile on his face as he circled the bases and crossed home plate as the winning run.

After the game, someone retrieved the ball and gave it to us. Normally, Mike and I would have gone home and played catch with the ball and hit it around until it turned into one big wad of string. But this ball became a trophy. My wife wrote the date on it and these descriptive words:

"Home Run – Last At Bat in Little League – City Championship – North Cambridge 8, Central 6"

The ball was then placed on the mantle with our kids' other trophies and awards. For the next several years, no matter where we lived, that ball was packed up and mounted on the family trophy case.

One of those stops was New York, where I was the head coach at St. John's University. During the 1999 basketball season, the team was staying in its normal hotel the night before a home game when I received a phone call from my friend Jason Togneri. I like to refer to Jason as Forrest Gump because he would always call me from the strangest places and put the most random but highly influential people on the phone to talk to me. On one occasion, he put me on the phone with Hall of Fame horse trainer Bob Baffert as he was saddling his horse for the Kentucky Derby. This call was no different.

"Coach, coach!" Jason said. "I've got somebody who wants to talk to you."

"Listen Jason," I replied. "I've got a big game at the Garden tomorrow. Can we do it another time?"

"No, no," he said. "You've got to talk to this guy now."

So I took the call and I tried to be as nice as I could.

"Hey coach, this is Matt," a man on the other end said.

"Matt who?" I asked.

"Matt Damon," he replied.

"Listen!" I quickly shot back. "Let's not play around. I don't have time for this."

"No, no coach!" he insisted. "This is really Matt Damon! I want you to know that I've been following you and Mike, and I'm really proud of you guys."

Matt and Ben Affleck had been in my gym class at Cambridge Rindge and Latin where they developed their acting chops alongside my daughter Dana and the school's drama team, so his story and his voice rang true.

"I've never told anybody this before," he continued. "When I was in little league, I was a pretty good pitcher. My dad was sure I would pitch for the Red Sox some day. When I was 12 years old, I was pitching in the city championship. I was throwing my best stuff and this kid comes up to bat and hits the ball out of the park. It was your son Mike. When I went home that day, my dad says, 'Hey Matt, maybe baseball's not your game.' So I started to mess around with acting and guess what, I'm doing pretty good today."

A few years later, I discovered that old baseball while unpacking some boxes after our move to Florida. It suddenly dawned on me. This ball that our family had kept for over two decades took on a whole new meaning. It certainly represented a lasting memory for our family, but I can imagine that ball meant even more to Matt Damon. He pitched that ball in a little league baseball game and in the process experienced a game changing moment that would immeasurably change his life for the better.

One Shot

In 1985, I was still coaching at Cambridge and aiming for another state championship. Our team was considered a heavy favorite to claim its fourth title in seven seasons. We no longer had Patrick Ewing, but instead featured another Jamaican born talent named Rumeal Robinson. He was a junior that year and would later go on to lead the University of Michigan to an NCAA Championship.

We faced Brockton High School in the semifinals. Brockton was noted for its football program, but they also had a great basketball team. Many believed that the winner of our game would likely win it all.

It was a classic back-and-forth game. With five seconds remaining, we took a one point lead and were one defensive stop away from victory. After a timeout, Brockton inbounded the ball and called another timeout. There were now only three seconds between us and another state championship.

I'll never forget the last play of that game. A Brockton player inbounded the ball to his teammate just over the half court line. He heaved the ball towards the basket. His shot went off the backboard and into the basket just before time expired.

The buzzer went off. Brockton won.

The players were devastated, and so was I. Thanks to the lessons I had learned from the great men I coached with and played for, I always tried to be gracious in defeat. This game was no different. Some of my postgame comments were widely publicized, and I ended up getting more positive coverage after the loss as the eventual champions got in their victory.

That offseason, we took the team on a cultural basketball trip to England and Wales. The day I got back to the United States, I received a call from Tom "Satch" Sanders, the legendary Celtics star and my old boss at Harvard.

"How would you like to be the next head coach at Boston University?" he asked.

Two days later, I was in a breakfast meeting with Boston's athletic director, Rick Taylor, and his assistant Larry Fudge. Two days after that, I was offered the job.

"Why me?" I asked.

One of the main reasons, Rick told me, was because of the way I handled myself after the loss against Brockton. I had already proven that I could coach, but it was my demeanor and the positive way I came across in the newspaper and on the television that sealed the deal. I had no idea of knowing it at the time, but weeks after it happened, that devastating loss turned out to be a game changing moment which would completely alter my coaching journey and my life.

One Sling

Few Bible stories have been recited or referenced more often than the classic battle between David and Goliath (1 Samuel 17). For many people who use the story in the context of a motivational speech or an inspirational message, David's victory over Goliath and the Israelites subsequent defeat of the Philistine army is the apex, and for good reason. It's an incredible ending to the greatest under-dog story of all time. The idea of a little shepherd boy defeating a hulking giant is enough to get everyone, from the locker room to the boardroom, excited.

I contend, however, that what happened before and after the big battle is even *more* significant to our everyday lives. Before David boldly accepted Goliath's challenge, he already knew God had king-sized plans for his life. That was confirmed the day the prophet Samuel anointed him (1 Samuel 16:1-13) and was reconfirmed in those times he protected his flock by single-handedly killing a lion and a bear (1 Samuel 17:34-36).

David's destiny was further solidified when he killed the giant. So when it was time for him to take his rightful place on the throne, he had the confidence and the courage to become the leader he was called to be.

His game changing moment may have been when he slung that

pebble into Goliath's forehead, but it didn't mean much until the purpose behind that moment had been fulfilled. David not only recognized his game changing moment; he chose to embrace it and allowed it to lead him into his destiny.

Everybody Needs A Game Changing Moment

Game changing moments can be wrapped up in glorious victories, like David's defeat of Goliath, or painful defeats, like Matt Damon's ill-fated pitch to my son Mike or the half-court shot that dashed my Cambridge team's championship hopes. Sometimes they can even be tied to tragic events.

Other times, however, these defining moments might simply be represented as disappointments or doors that are closed. But as Julie Andrews' character Maria famously said in *The Sound of Music*, "When the Lord closes a door, somewhere He opens a window."

Whatever the case may be, here are three simple keys to help us all deal with the game changing moments in our lives:

1. Be prepared: Don't be surprised when a game changing moment takes place in your life. Even if things are going smoothly at the time, it's inevitable that something is going to shake things up. Make sure your feet are firmly planted on a solid foundation so that sudden changes don't slow you down or knock you out.

"Truly my soul finds rest in God; my salvation comes from Him. Truly He is my rock and my salvation; He is my fortress, I will never be shaken." (Psalm 62:1-2/NIV)

2. Be hopeful: This is especially important when a game changing moment is the result of a discouraging or disappointing outcome. Remember that even bad things can lead to great things if we keep our hope in God's promises.

"And we know that in all things God works for the good of those who love him, who have been called according to his purpose." (Romans 8:28/NIV)

3. Be courageous: In situations where a game changing moment creates a big decision, it's important to keep fear and doubt at bay. This is only possible when we rely on the supernatural courage that comes from a trusting relationship with God.

"Have I not commanded you? Be strong and courageous. Do not be afraid; do not be discouraged, for the LORD your God will be with you wherever you go." (Joshua 1:9/NIV)

It's not a matter of if but when. Change *will* come, and only you have the power to allow it to set forth the positive transformation that God wants to implement in your life.

Everybody needs a game changing moment.

Study Questions

1. Do you generally welcome or resist change? Explain.

2. Have you ever experienced a game changing moment? If so, was it a victorious moment (like David's defeat of Goliath) or a disappointing moment (like Matt Damon's home run pitch or the Cambridge team's tough loss)?

3. Were you immediately aware of how that game changing moment was going to redirect your life or was it something that became evident much later? Explain.

4. Of the three keys to facing change listed (being prepared, being hopeful, or being courageous), which one has caused you the most difficulty when a game changing moment has come along? Explain.

5. What are some specific ways that your life might be different should you decide to more enthusiastically embrace the game changing moments that come your way?

6. What are some things you feel like you need to do to be, A) better prepared, B) more hopeful, and C) more courageous, when dealing with game changing moments?

Prayer

Lord, prepare my heart for whatever game changing moments You might send my way. Fill me with the hope I need to move forward when I am facing difficult transitions in life. Give me the courage to embrace change and not to allow fear and doubt to keep me from fulfilling my destiny. I trust that You have a plan for my life and that You have worked out everything for my good. Amen.

CHAPTER TWELVE

THE CRISCO KID
Everybody Needs An Encourager

"Our chief want is someone who will inspire us to be what we know we could be." – Ralph Waldo Emerson

I wish I could tell you I was a great athlete and that I used my athletic ability to make a career and a name for myself in basketball, but I wasn't.

Fortunately, there were people on both ends of the spectrum who motivated me to overachieve. On one end, there were some neighborhood kids who told me I wasn't very good, but on the other end of that equation, there were people like my mother, my older brother Richard and my sister Trudy who always told me I could try to be anything I wanted to be. I was also blessed to have mentors like my little league baseball coach Stretch Headley, my youth basketball coach Rindge Jefferson and grade school teachers like Mrs. Key who encouraged me to always try to do my best and made me feel special.

Then there was my best friend Gene Ward, whose brother was given the nickname Buzzy because of his short legs and arms. One day, while playing a game of touch football with my buddies Bull, Ducky, Fish and Leader, Buzzy gave me a nickname of my own: Crisco.

"Buzzy, why you calling me Crisco?" I asked.

"Because I like ya," he replied. "And I don't want to call ya fatso."

To this day, if you go back to my old neighborhood in Cambridge, Mass., nicknamed "The Coast" because of its proximity to the Charles River, some people won't know me as Mike. They will know me as Crisco.

From a very young age, I loved sports, especially basketball and baseball. I was never a great athlete, and quite often I would be the last player selected for our pickup games. One thing I was good at, though, even at a young age, was spotting talent and putting a good team together. Throughout my childhood and my teen years, I became a key member on most of the teams I played on because I was competitive, I had natural leadership qualities, and I helped my teams win. It was a lot easier for me to tell people what to do than to do it myself, so it's not a surprise that I eventually made a living doing that very thing as a basketball coach.

No. 54

Like most Americans, I've always had an affinity for the underdog. But for me, it's been a very personal connection due to my experience as that chubby kid known as Crisco. Perhaps that's why I've always enjoyed proving people wrong. That was the case during my time as an athlete and it continued throughout my coaching career. My admiration for underdogs even translated into my recruiting strategy and would often help me find athletes who were overlooked and undervalued. I took pride in trying to see potential where others did not. I saw what could be, not just what was.

Early in my career as head coach at George Washington University, I attended an AAU tournament where I was scouting some potential recruits. The size and length of those high school athletes was incredible. But there was one player in particular that stood out. His name was Shawnta Rogers.

Shawnta was one of the most electrifying players I had ever seen. He was fast. He was quick. He was strong. He was a fierce competitor. All I could hear from the other coaches, though, was that he wasn't tall enough to play Division I basketball. How could a five-foot guy play and win in the Atlantic 10 Conference? What everyone failed to measure was the size of Shawnta's heart and his ability to lead and inspire his teammates.

During my coaching career, I always thought that I was a little bit of a promoter. The legendary Boston Celtics coach Red

Auerbach was one of my mentors and I often tried to take a page out of his playbook and apply one of the many lessons he taught me. At the end of Shawnta's sophomore year, I called him into my office for a meeting.

"Shawnta, every time people see you play, I want them to know it's you and how special you are. So I would like you to wear number 53."

Shawnta immediately picked up on the symbolism of my plan and rebuffed the idea.

"Coach, I'm 5-5," he said.

"Shawnta, you're not 5-5. You're 5-3. C'mon over here. Stand against the wall."

My usually energetic point guard was suddenly not so enthusiastic as I measured his height just like I used to measure myself when I was a kid trying to grow taller. I was right. He was only 5-3, but I could tell Shawnta didn't want to relent. So I came up with a solution.

"Okay Shawnta. We'll compromise. Let's meet in the middle. How about if you wear number 54? Every time people see that jersey number, they'll know it's you."

He agreed. The next season, that number became very significant in college basketball. A lot of people remembered No. 54. That is a *big* number on a little guy's back. But Shawnta played the game of basketball like few other people his size had ever played. I think he was as good as any undersized athlete to ever step on the court.

As a junior, Shawnta led the Colonials to an Atlantic 10 championship and a trip to the NCAA Tournament. He averaged 15 points and five assists per game. During his senior year, Shawnta averaged 20 points, seven assists and four rebounds per game and led the nation in steals per game with 3.55. He was named MVP of the Atlantic 10 Conference over 6-10 forward Lamar Odom from Rhode Island University, who went on to have a stellar NBA career with the Los Angeles Lakers.

That same year, Shawnta won the Frances Pomeroy Naismith Award as the best NCAA player under six feet tall. Shawnta's size kept him from playing in the NBA, but he did have a spectacular decade-long career in France where he was later named to the country's Basketball Hall of Fame.

Perhaps the most interesting aspect of Shawnta's basketball success is the way he handled himself in the biggest games. When he was a kid growing up in Baltimore, he dreamed about playing for his state school, the University of Maryland. Head coach Gary Williams knew Shawnta was an elite high school athlete, but he didn't think he was big enough to play in the Atlantic Coast Conference. Shawnta came to George Washington instead.

In December of 1997, our team took part in the annual BB&T Classic, held at the Verizon Center in Washington D.C. It was Shawnta's junior season, and he was really starting to come into his own as one of the conference's top players. As fate would have it, our opponent in the championship game was Maryland. Gary Williams believed that his full court press could stop any team. Shawnta knew there was no press that could stop him.

For 40 minutes, Shawnta dribbled through and around the Terrapins' vaunted press and GWU came away with the 70-66 victory and the championship trophy. It was rewarding to see him play so well against the program for which he once dreamed of playing. Shawnta certainly proved them wrong.

Proving God Right

It's easy to get caught up in a prideful attitude when we try to prove others wrong and prove ourselves right. The true message to be found in Shawnta's story is part of a much bigger picture. And it doesn't have anything to do with us at all! Instead, it's all about what's on the inside.

In 1 Samuel 16, we find the iconic account of a young shepherd boy named David. If you had asked his father Jesse or his older brothers, David wasn't supposed to amount to much. Even the divinely appointed judge Samuel had a hard time believing that Jesse's youngest son could one day become the King of Judah.

In the end, however, David turned out to be bigger than a giant.

The story of how David defeated the Philistine warrior Goliath has usually been portrayed in books, in art, and in film as the ultimate underdog story, someone small and insignificant overcoming the greatest of odds to win a battle in the unlikeliest of circumstances.

When David slayed Goliath and led the army to victory, not only did David prove the naysayers wrong, he proved that God was right. The world says a lot of things to discourage you, just like the Philistines said to David and like what the majority of the basketball world said to Shawnta:

"You're too small."
"You're not smart enough."
"You're unattractive."
"You have no purpose."
"You're not a good person."
"You're too weak."
"You're too poor."
"You've made too many mistakes."
"You're worthless."

But through His encouraging Word, God tells you something completely different:

"I am bigger than anything you'll ever face." (Matthew 19:26, John 16:33)
   "I can give you wisdom." (Proverbs 2:6, James 1:5)
   "I made you in My image." (Genesis 1:27, Psalm 139:14)
   "I have a plan for your life." (Jeremiah 29:11, Matthew 5:16-17)
   "I am your righteousness." (Romans 1:17, 1 Corinthians 1:30)
   "I am your strength." (Isaiah 41:10, Philippians 4:13)
   "I am your provider." (Matthew 6:26, Philippians 4:19)
   "I paid the price for you." (John 3:16, Romans 5:8)
   "You are worth *everything* to Me." (Matthew 6:25-34, Romans 8:32)

When we go against the grain and resist the temptation to listen to what the world says about us, then that allows God to use us for His purpose and for His glory. We can achieve great things and not only prove that the doubters were wrong, but more importantly prove God was right. Our victories become a testimony to the truth found in His Word and the love inside of us.

Everybody Needs An Encourager

So what does this mean for us today? What is the lesson we should take from a lowly shepherd boy like David or an undersized basketball player like Shawnta Rogers?

Both of those young men, like so many others who have over-achieved in this world, accomplished great things because they had someone who believed in them and someone who encouraged them to chase after their dreams. I can certainly relate. One of the main reasons any of us are able to overcome the odds and achieve success is because of the encouraging people God places in our lives at just the right time.

Jesus Christ modeled this principle for us throughout the New Testament Gospels. He encouraged His disciples to step out of their comfort zone and stretch themselves for the sake of the ministry. Before Jesus was crucified, He told the disciples that a comforter and encourager would be coming to help them after He was gone. (John 14:16-17) Because of His empowering words, they had the faith to perform miracles and lay the foundation for the early Christian church (Acts 2).

We still have access to that same Holy Spirit today (Romans 8:11). He comforts us in times when we are filled with fear and doubt. He encourages us in times when our life's circumstances frustrate and discourage us.

And then, as we are encouraged and lifted up, God calls us to encourage others (1 Thessalonians 5:11). He asks us to be there for those who need a shoulder to lean on, for those who need an ear to listen, and for those who need a smiling face to tell them things like "everything is going to be okay," and "things will get better," and "this too will pass," and "God doesn't make mistakes," and "trust in God" and "embrace His word."

We must see others through a different lens. We need to see others the way *God* sees them.

Back when I was known as Crisco, I didn't look like a Division I basketball coach. Shawnta Rogers didn't look like a Division I basketball player. David didn't look like a king. That kid down the street might not look like a doctor or a teacher. That recovering alcoholic might not look like a pastor or a business owner. But God can take someone that doesn't look like much and do something special with him or her.

Who knows? You might be the very person who can build them up and empower them to do great things for God.

Everybody needs an encourager.

Study Questions

1. Name some people who have encouraged you throughout your life? How did their encouraging words make a difference?

2. What are some obstacles you have faced (physical, emotional, financial, etc.)? Have you been able to overcome those on your own or have you needed to rely on others to help you get through them?

3. Can you personally relate to any of the stories told in this chapter (Coach Jarvis, Shawnta Rogers or King David) and a time when you felt like an underdog? How so?

4. What are some difficult things the world, or society, has said to you? Take a few moments to find a scripture in the Bible that counters those negative declarations and write it down. You might also think about some encouragements that you have read in a book, seen in an inspirational movie, heard in a song, or heard in a sermon, and write those down as well.

5. Can you think of a time when your encouraging words made a difference in someone else's life?

6. What are some other ways you can encourage and build up others?

Prayer

Lord, thank You for the encouraging promises found in Your Word. Thank You for allowing Your Holy Spirit to comfort and encourage me in those times when I have experienced fear and doubt. Give me the boldness and courage to step out and find others I can encourage when they too are experiencing fear and doubt. I want to be a vessel that You can use to help others fulfill their divine purpose in life. Amen.

CHAPTER THIRTEEN

CURTAIN CALL
Everybody Needs To Play A Role

"Each of us has a role to play, and every role is important. There is no small service to God. It all matters." – Rick Warren

Life is one giant exercise in teamwork. From an early age, we are all thrust into various groups and play for teams that must work together in order to be successful. Teamwork starts with our family, progresses into the classroom, shows up on the ball field, and graduates into the workplace, the church, and the community.

Within those team dynamics are various jobs and responsibilities. Some roles are highly visible, while other roles are not visible at all, but without all the roles working together, it is virtually impossible to achieve a common goal.

Best Supporting Actress/Academy Award Winning Mom

My daughter Dana was born 18 months after my son Mike Jr. She wasn't into athletics like her brother. Instead, Dana showed an interest in the arts at a very young age. Because our kids were into different things, the best way to give them the attention they deserved was for me to spend a lot of time with Mike and for my wife Connie to spend a lot of time with Dana. Then, we would all attend everyone's events as a family.

Dana and her friends became involved in dance. She loved getting dressed up and made up to go to her many dance recitals. Dana also took piano lessons at her grandmother's house from Mr. Ford, who taught my wife Connie how to play when she was eight years old. Dana was a good singer and dancer, but she really excelled at the piano.

When Dana was in the third grade at St. John's parochial school, she gave a one-person performance that featured the music of Stephen Foster. I often tell people it wasn't Michael Jordan, Larry Bird or Patrick Ewing that put on the greatest individual performance I ever saw. It was my daughter singing and playing the piano at that third-grade recital.

When Dana attended Cambridge Rindge and Latin High School, she was a member of one of the best drama teams in the country and performed in the school's brand new amphitheater. Dana always tried out for parts in the many plays and musicals, but on numerous occasions she would come home disappointed. She was happy to be on the team but frustrated that she never could get the lead role.

As her dad and number one fan, I couldn't understand how my multi-talented daughter couldn't be a starter, so to speak, in the acting world. After attending two or three musicals, it started to make sense. Dana's situation was similar to what it might have been like for me as a young basketball player trying to play on the same team with Michael Jordan, Scottie Pippen and those great Chicago Bulls players. Dana was on the same team with a group of young people who would go on to become world-class actors on television, in film, and on Broadway.

At the top of the list was a kid named Matt Damon. I knew him as the little boy who used to play Little League baseball against my son Mike, but the world now knows him as the star of major blockbuster films such as *Good Will Hunting, Saving Private Ryan, Ocean's Eleven,* and *The Bourne Identity.*

His best friend was a California transplant named Ben Affleck. He also starred in *Good Will Hunting* and other box office smash hits like *Armageddon, Pearl Harbor, Argo* and *Gone Girl.*

Max Dietch, now known as Max Cassella, was also on that drama team with Dana. He is best known for his role as Vinnie on the classic hit TV show "Doogie Howser M.D." and for his supporting part as Benny Fazio in "The Sopranos." Max has also spent time on Broadway in "The Lion King" and "The Music Man."

Coach Jarvis (top row, far left) with his first team, the Newton North (MA) sophomore squad in 1967.

Coach Jarvis (top row, far left) with the 1973-74 Harvard University freshman team.

Mike and Connie Jarvis on their wedding day, September 9, 1967.

Patrick Ewing, age 14 (center), with Mike Jarvis Jr., age eight (left), and Dana Jarvis, age six (right) at Coach Jarvis' Shoot Straight co-ed youth basketball program in 1976.

Coach Jarvis (far right) talks strategy with Patrick Ewing (far left), assistant coach Vin Mili (right) and the Cambridge Rindge and Latin Warriors boy's basketball team in a timeout during the 1981 season.

Coach Jarvis and the 1979 state championship Cambridge Rindge and Latin team pose on the steps of the U.S. Capitol Building with Cambridge resident Speaker of the House Tip O'Neill (bottom right).

Coach Jarvis, son Mike Jr., Patrick Ewing and the Cambridge Rindge and Latin boys basketball team celebrate after winning the 1979 Massachusetts state championship.

Coach Jarvis and the 1979 CRLS team meet with U.S. Senator Ted Kennedy.

Coach Jarvis sports his 1979 state championship sweater in a picture for the CRLS student newspaper, the *Rindge Register.*

From left to right: Mike Jarvis Jr., and Coach Jarvis with members of the 1981 McDonald's All-American East squad Manuel Forrest, Milt Wagner, Adrian Branch, Buzz Peterson and Michael Jordan (kneeling).

The 1981 McDonald's All-American East squad (from left to right): Coach Jarvis, Buzz Peterson, Milt Wagner, Eugene McDowell, Patrick Ewing, Bill Wennington, Adrian Branch, Manuel Forrest, Chris Mullin, Jeff Adkins, Michael Jordan, and assistant coach Mike Jarvis Jr.

Coach Jarvis argues a call from the sidelines at Boston University's Walter Brown Arena.

Coach Jarvis' 1989-90 Boston team hoists the North Atlantic Conference championship trophy. (From left to right): Scott White, Steve Key, Sitirois Manolopulus, Francis Kalitsi and Mark Daley.

Coach Jarvis (fourth from right) with his 1985-86 Boston University Terriers squad that won 21 games and received an invitation to play in the National Invitational Tournament (NIT).

Coach Jarvis addresses the media ahead of George Washington's appearance in the 1993 NCAA Tournament.

Coach Jarvis (right) with legendary Boston Celtics head coach Red Auerbach (left).

Coach Jarvis gives his St. John's squad some instruction from the sidelines during a nationally televised game on CBS.

George Washington point guard #54 Shawnta Rogers (center) led Coach Jarvis' Colonials squad to three NCAA Tournament appearances (1996, 1998 and 1999).

Assistant coach Mike Jarvis Jr. (left) and Coach Jarvis (right) talk strategy in preparation for another St. John's game.

Coach Jarvis and his St. John's squad listens intently as assistant coach Mike Jarvis Jr., shares the game strategy for that evening's game.

Coach Jarvis (right) with St. John's guard Erick Barkley (left) during the second half of the 2000 Big East Conference championship game. Barkley's left wrist was inadvertently cut and then taped up during a halftime locker room incident.

Coach Jarvis (front row, third from left) with his 1998-99 St. John's squad that reached the NCAA Tournament's Elite Eight and featured future NBA first-round draft picks Ron Artest (back row, third from left) and Erick Barkley (front row, third from right). Also pictured, Mike Jarvis Jr., (middle row, second from right).

Coach Jarvis (left) and former Connecticut head coach Jim Calhoun (right) have a pre-game chat.

Coach Jarvis (right) accompanies hip hop recording artist Jay-Z to center court at St. John's Midnight Madness celebration in 2001.

Coach Jarvis (center right) welcomes President Bill Clinton (center left) into the St. John's locker room after a victory at Madison Square Garden in 2000.

Coach Jarvis cuts down the net after St. John's 2003 NIT championship in Madison Square Garden.

Coach Jarvis and the St. John's players and staff after winning the 2003 NIT championship in Madison Square Garden.

Coach Jarvis (center left) and his 2003 NIT championship team from St. John's walk through the crowded New York Stock Exchange on their way to ringing the opening bell.

Coach Jarvis (left) chats with legendary New York Knicks player Willis Reed (right) before a St. John's game at Madison Square Garden.

ESPN commentator Jay Bilas interviews Coach Jarvis (center) and Anthony Glover (right) after a St. John's victory.

ESPN commentator Bill Raftery (right) interviews Coach Jarvis (left) and Lavar Postell (center) after a St. John's victory.

Coach Jarvis (center) instructs his St. John's team during a timeout.

Coach Jarvis (right) with Hall of Fame Duke head coach Mike Krzyewski (left).

Coach Jarvis (center) with former St. John's and NBA star Mark Jackson (left) and legendary St. John's head coach Lou Carneseca (right).

Coach Jarvis (center left) and Michael Jordan (center right) with Ed Manetta (far left) and Don Hazelton (far right) at the Metropolitan Club in New York during a St. John's fundraiser.

Coach Jarvis (right) during a game in Hawaii where he led the 2000 USA Basketball Men's Select Team against Vince Carter (left) and the US Men's National Team.

Coach Jarvis (center) with former NBA stars Jayson Williams (left) and Chris Mullin (right) at the Inner City Games in New York.

(From left to right): Daughter Dana Shaiyen, grandsons Ian and Geoffrey Shaiyen, wife Connie, and Mike Jarvis Sr., holding grandson Noah Shaiyen.

(From left to right): Daughter-in-law Jennifer Jarvis, Mike Jarvis Sr., holding granddaughter Delaney Jarvis, wife Connie holding grandson Madison Jarvis, and son Mike Jarvis Jr.

Coach Jarvis in his trademark catcher's stance on the sideline during a St. John's game.

There also was Traci Bingham, who went on to star in "Baywatch," and Fanshen Cox, who has appeared on numerous TV shows and films and performed a one-woman show called "One Drop of Love" that her good friends Matt and Ben produced.

Dana never got a lead role because of the incredible depth of talent that surrounded her. We did our best to encourage her to be the best supporting actress she could be, and that's exactly what she did. Dana never let her disappointments interfere with her passion and zeal for performing and contributing to the success of the team. She was the equivalent of the sixth man, who comes off the bench to contribute valuable minutes to the overall effort.

While attending Boston University, Dana still had dreams of acting, but they never panned out. That didn't stop her from having a great run as a student. She graduated from the liberal arts program before moving on to The George Washington University where she earned a master's degree in the international tourism program. Dana remained in Washington D.C. and built a successful career as an event planner with Festive Foods.

Dana found her true calling and what God really wanted her to be when she took on her greatest role ever. She became an Academy Award winning mom to her sons Geoffrey and Ian. Then, after 10 years of raising her two boys, she decided she wanted another child. Dana and her husband Hubert brought Noah into the family.

Shortly after the birth of her first child, Dana told Connie that she wanted to be the best mother God ever created. She wanted to play that role to perfection, and that is worth more than any success that Hollywood or Broadway could ever offer. The most thunderous applause received during a curtain call can never replace the gratification of knowing that she is fulfilling God's calling for her life.

The Sixth Man

Cambridge was a great city to grow up in. There was a real sense of community, and everyone had the opportunity to receive a quality education and pursue the American dream. Every community had its own recreation facility; ours was called the Cambridge Community Center. That's where I learned to play basketball from Rindge Jefferson, a great teacher, mentor and role model.

Coach Jefferson put teams together and on occasion would take us to play in exhibition contests before the Celtics games. Here I was, at the age of 10, playing on the world famous parquet floor at the Boston Garden. Afterwards, I would stay with the team and watch my heroes take the court, future Hall of Fame athletes like Bill Russell, Bob Cousy, Bill Sharman, the Jones boys, and their legendary coach Red Auerbach.

One day back at the community center, a big guy walked into our gym. I immediately recognized him as one of those Celtic greats.

"That's Sam Jones," I said to myself.

I may have been the little fat kid nicknamed Crisco, but that didn't stop me one bit. I went right over to him and started what must have seemed like an awkward conversation to anyone else hanging around.

"Hey! You're Sam Jones!" I blurted out.

"No, it's not me," he replied. "I'm not Sam Jones."

"You are too Sam Jones!" I insisted. "I saw you play at the Garden."

"No, no, no! That's my brother," he responded.

"Let's play a game of 21," I challenged, with a basketball in my hand.

"I don't play," he answered back. "My brother's the basketball player. But I'll play you a game if you let me shoot first."

I gave him the ball and never touched it again. He never missed a shot and I never got to take a turn. After three consecutive shutouts, he flipped the ball back to me.

"By the way, I *am* Sam Jones," he said with a smile as he walked away.

Later in life, I got to know Sam better through my relationships with Coach Red Auerbach and Sam's Celtics teammate Tom "Satch" Sanders. When teaching my players how to shoot the bank shot, I always talked about Sam Jones because no one could do it better than him, and he had nine championship rings to prove it.

My first meeting with Sam was humorous and his penchant for the fundamentals of shooting was a help to my coaching career. But that's not what made him special. Sam played for many great Celtics teams, yet early in his career he came off the bench. In today's game, players in his situation likely would have gone somewhere else to be the star. Instead, Sam accepted his role as the sixth man and won championship after championship in Boston. He eventually became a starter, made it into the Hall of Fame, and was recognized as one of the game's 50 greatest players.

Unknown Soldiers

In the Bible, we often emphasize the stories of great leaders like Abraham, Moses, Joshua, Esther, David, Solomon and Daniel. Yet behind the scenes and often unidentified were many others who played less visible roles that were by no means insignificant.

Perhaps one of the best examples of such an important position was the armor bearer. These courageous men were servants who carried additional weapons for commanders such as Abimelech, Saul, Jonathan and David. Armor bearers were also charged with finishing off wounded enemies with clubs or swords. If a commander was about to be captured, he would often order his armor bearer to kill him in order to avoid humiliation and torture.

We never read the names of armor bearers in these biblical stories, but we do know that they were very important despite their lack of recognition. In 1 Samuel 14, King Saul's son Jonathan decided to go on an unauthorized military excursion. At the time, the Israelites were entrenched in battle against the Philistines.

After approaching an enemy outpost, Jonathan told the young armor bearer his plan to which he replied:

"Do all that you have in mind. Go ahead. I am with you heart and soul." (1 Samuel 14:7/NIV)

Jonathan courageously climbed up a hill to where the Philistines were camped. Together, he and his armor bearer killed 20 soldiers in an area that covered nearly half an acre. Jonathan surely received much praise for his effort, but it was the bravery and commitment of the armor bearer who was willing to play his supporting role that made the victory possible.

Everybody Needs To Play A Role

For my daughter Dana, the concept of faithfully playing a role was learned during her time as an actress and then utilized to a greater extent as a mother. Sam Jones played his role as sixth man to perfection and used the experience to eventually become one of the stars. The Old Testament armor bearers may not have received historical fame, but there is no doubt that many battles would not have been won without their courage and bravery.

All of these stories provide perfect parallels to my time as a head coach. So often there were players who didn't want to come off the bench. They wanted the attention that came from being a starter. They didn't see the value of playing a lesser role, but the young athletes who understood the concept were some of my hardest working and most appreciated players.

Whether it's on the basketball court, in the home or on the battlefield of war, no effort will ever be successful if each individual on the team doesn't fully embrace and play his or her role. In the New Testament, the Apostle Paul had a lot to say about the topic of working together and the importance of each part of a team. In fact, he cleverly used the metaphor of the human body.

"Even so the body is not made up of one part but of many. Now if the foot should say, 'Because I am not the hand, I do not belong to the body,' it would not for that reason stop being part of the body. And if the ear should say, 'Because I am not the eye, I do not belong to the body,' it would not for that reason stop being part of the body. If the whole body were an eye, where would the sense of hearing be? If the whole body were an ear, where would the sense of smell be?

But in fact God has placed the parts in the body, every one of them, just as He wanted them to be." (1 Corinthians 12:14-18/NIV)

From an athletic standpoint, it's just as clear. If my team had an incredible center but no point guard to bring the ball down the court and create offense through his passing, how would that team have any chance at success? The same holds true in baseball where a pitcher can't do his job without a catcher behind the plate, or in football where a quarterback is useless without a center to snap him the ball.

We should value the roles that are often overlooked or deemed less important. For instance, my teams would not have been able to practice if the custodian didn't open the gym and turn the lights on. No matter how unimportant you think your job is, it really is important. You would be missed if you didn't show up.

Here are four simple things we can all do to more fully embrace this concept:

1. Know Your Role: First of all, you have to have an understanding of your gifting and your calling in life. You can only do this through honest self-assessment and with the help of others around you who will truthfully help you identify your strengths and weaknesses.

"For by the grace given me I say to every one of you: Do not think of yourself more highly than you ought, but rather think of yourself with sober judgment, in accordance with the faith God has distributed to each of you." (Romans 12:3/NIV)

2. Appreciate Your Role: You need to know and truly believe that your role is important and has value. Having this attitude will make it easier for you to get up and perform your job with renewed joy and a right perspective.

"There are different kinds of gifts, but the same Spirit distributes them. There are different kinds of service, but the same Lord. There are different kinds of workings, but in all of them and in everyone it is the same God at work." (1 Corinthians 12:4-6/NIV)

3. Respect Others In Their Roles: It's hard sometimes not to be jealous of others who are in the spotlight and in higher positions of authority, but if we are to be successful in our communities, in our churches and in our families, we must commit to working together for the greater good.

"Now we ask you, brothers and sisters, to acknowledge those who work hard among you, who care for you in the Lord and who admonish you. Hold them in the highest regard in love because of their work. Live in peace with each other." (1 Thessalonians 5:12-13/NIV)

4. Give The Best For Your Role: Show up every day. Give your best at all times. There is no substitute for hard work. Whatever role you have been called to play, do it to the best of your ability. Do it for the team. Most importantly, do it for God's glory.

"Work willingly at whatever you do, as though you were working for the Lord rather than for people." (Colossians 3:23/NLT)

We all have desires. We all have goals. We all have dreams. But God knows what is best for each of us. When we understand that we are all part of a much bigger plan, we can more genuinely and freely engage in the calling that has been placed on our lives. So much more can be accomplished when we commit to the responsibilities we have each been given.

Everybody needs to play a role.

Study Questions

1. Describe a time in your life when you weren't able to accomplish a goal or fulfill a dream because someone else was in the position that you were pursuing. How did that make you feel?

2. Are you someone who usually feels the need to be in charge or are you just as comfortable playing a secondary role within a team effort? If you're not chosen as the leader or captain, do you still give your best effort, or do you become lax and disinterested?

3. Why do you think so many people aren't satisfied with their job, their role, their responsibilities, etc.? Can you relate to some of those feelings?

4. Do you feel like you have a good grasp on your role in various stations of your life (i.e. family, work, church, the community)? Are you satisfied with those roles or do you sometimes wish they were different? Explain.

5. Do you ever struggle to appreciate your role? If so, why do you think that's the case?

6. What are some things you can change today that might help you better understand, accept and more enthusiastically play the various roles that you have been given for this particular time in your life?

Prayer

Lord, thank You for giving me a role to play in my family, my church, my workplace and my community. I want to fully embrace my responsibilities and use my gifts and abilities for the greater good of those around me. Give me humility in those times when I am called to lead as well as those times when I am called to follow. No matter what role I am asked to play, give me the strength to do my best, not for the praise of men, but for Your glory. Amen.

CHAPTER FOURTEEN

BUZZER BEATER
Everybody Needs To Make A Decision

"When you have to make a choice and don't make it, that is in itself a choice." – William James

Some decisions in life are easy. Things like what to wear to work or what to have for lunch don't require too much thought, and the consequences are relatively insignificant.

Other decisions can be very difficult. Choices that involve important aspects of our lives such as our jobs, our relationships and our finances are often quite challenging and usually have a long-term impact.

My dad wasn't the best at making good decisions because he didn't have to. As a youngster growing up, my grandmother and grandfather gave him whatever he wanted. Dad never had to work for anything, and whenever he messed up, they were there to bail him out. He was spoiled and never had to make decisions or pay the consequences for his choices. Important things like being on time, keeping your word, or finishing assigned tasks were not part of his DNA.

To make matters worse, he could never make up his mind if he wanted to act like a responsible husband and father. In too many instances, he chose *not* to make a choice, which, as the English philosopher William James said was, "in itself a choice."

So when he was dying of pancreatic cancer, I grew increasingly concerned about his spiritual wellbeing. I traveled from New York back to Cambridge as often as I could to see him while he was physically withering away. I asked my brother-in-law Richard Richardson, a senior member of the ministerial staff and assistant to the senior pastor at St. Paul A.M.E. Church, to come with me and minister to my dad. As they continued to spend more time together, Richard would report back to me that my dad was getting close to accepting Jesus as his Lord and Savior.

But just like the seconds on the clock at a basketball game, time was running out.

Last Second Shot

In early 1993, I was in my second year as the head coach at George Washington University. By early February, we had compiled a 10-8 record, which was actually pretty good for the program at that time. Three days before we were set to travel to New Jersey and play Rutgers, I dreamed I was coaching in a game and used a last-second play that I had learned from legendary NBA coach Hubie Brown at a Nike basketball clinic the previous spring.

The next day at practice, I told the team about my dream. After we warmed up, I introduced our new play. Since the play didn't have a name, I decided to call it Hubie. It was a play we would use in a situation where we needed to go the length of the court for a last-second desperation shot to either tie or win the game. For the next two days, we spent the last 10 minutes of each practice on our new play Hubie.

Lo and behold, four days later, on February 2, 1993, we found ourselves down two points against Rutgers with just 1.8 seconds left on the clock. With the ball underneath our own goal, 94 feet away, I called timeout and brought the team over to the bench.

"You know what guys?" I said. "We're gonna run the new play. We're gonna run Hubie."

After going over the play one last time, the team headed back out to court. Billy Brigham took the ball from the referee. He took two steps to his right then changed direction as he ran off point guard Alvin Pearsal's screen along the baseline. Billy threw a high arching baseball pass that sailed over the outstretched arms of the defense and into the hands of our seven-foot center Yinka Dare, who was positioned in the lane. Yinka caught the ball and laid it in to tie the game just before the time on the clock expired and the buzzer sounded.

We went on to win the game 105-100 in double overtime.

After one of the most memorable victories in my coaching career, I boarded the bus and was told that my brother-in-law was on the phone. My fears were confirmed when Richard told me that my dad had just passed away.

Although the news wasn't unexpected, it broke my heart nonetheless. My sadness, however, turned to joy when Richard told me that my dad had accepted Jesus that morning. Our team hit a buzzer beater to win a basketball game, but my dad made a buzzer beater too. And his would last forever. It was a wonderful feeling to know he had secured his eternal future and that I would see him again someday.

Our victory at Rutgers sparked a winning streak that propelled the school to its first NCAA Tournament in 32 years. Our Cinderella ride finally ended in a Sweet Sixteen loss in Seattle against Michigan's Fab Five. Maybe, just maybe, my dad was somehow connected with that miraculous buzzer beater.

Last Second Confession

The story of Jesus' crucifixion can be difficult to read. Some of the movie depictions, like *The Passion of the Christ*, can be even more difficult to watch. Yet in the midst of such a brutally violent scene, something amazing took place as Jesus hung on the cross and painfully neared His death. (Luke 23)

There were two criminals who had also been crucified that day. One was to His right and one was to His left.

"Father, forgive them, for they don't know what they are doing," Jesus prayed as the people mocked Him. (v. 34/NLT)

"He saved others," they said, "let Him save Himself if He is really God's Messiah, the Chosen One." (v. 35/NLT)

One of the criminals hanging next to him chimed in with the crowd.

"So you're the Messiah, are you? Prove it by saving yourself – and us, too, while you're at it!" (v. 39/NLT)

The criminal had made a decision. He looked at his dire situation on that cross, yet failed to see the opportunity that was staring him in the face. He chose to reject Jesus and enter eternity with Satan in hell.

But the other criminal could tell there was something different about Jesus and spoke up in His defense. He had probably heard the stories about this man who shared the Good News about His Father in Heaven and how He had performed many miracles throughout the land.

"Don't you fear God even when you have been sentenced to die? We deserve to die for our crimes, but this man hasn't done anything wrong." (vv. 40-41/NLT)

And then the criminal made a very important decision. He turned to Jesus with a simple request.

"Jesus, remember me when you come into your Kingdom." (v. 42/NLT)

For the criminal, there wasn't much time left, but it wasn't too late for him to change his eternal future. Jesus replied:

"I assure you today, you will be with me in paradise." (v. 43/NLT)

Everybody Needs To Make A Decision

It's never too late to make a decision. It's never too late to make a change. It might be the need to shake some bad habits or a desire to become spiritually stronger and more connected in a relationship with God.

Making a decision to change something is never easy. It takes a tremendous amount of courage. If it's a lifestyle change, it might require some hard questions followed by some honest assessments. What can I do to make this situation right? What can I do to make things better? What are my faults? What *needs* to change?

If you are having a hard time making a decision in your life, here are four things that might push you in the right direction:

1. Overcome your fear: Most of the time, decisions are not made because we are afraid of change or afraid of the unknown. I was fearful about writing this book. Would people actually read it? Would they care about what I had to say? At the end of the day, I had to overcome that fear and step out to do something new and unfamiliar to me. Overcome your fear and you can do the same.

"This is my command–be strong and courageous! Do not be afraid or discouraged. For the Lord your God is with you wherever you go." (Joshua 1:9/NLT)

2. Overcome your pride: There are a lot of ways pride can keep you from making a decision. It can keep you from asking someone for advice. It can also keep you from doing something different that might seem strange or out of the ordinary. Like fear, pride can kill progress and leave you paralyzed.

"When pride comes, then comes disgrace, but with humility comes wisdom." (Proverbs 11:2/NIV)

3. Weigh the cost: Making a decision should not be devoid of logic and common sense. This is where wise counsel and measured judgment comes into play. Ask someone you trust about your choices, write down the pros and cons, and then honestly assess the situation. Most importantly, ask God what He thinks. After all, He is the one opening and closing all the doors and directing your path.

"Fools think their own way is right, but the wise listen to others." (Proverbs 12:15/NLT)

4. Don't wait too long: There comes a time when you just have to make a decision. Once again, to reiterate William James' point, not making a choice is really a choice after all. And waiting too long to decide will put you in a rut from which you might not be able to escape. Instead, put your faith in God and He will help you make the right decision.

"Trust in the Lord with all your heart and lean not on your own understanding; in all your ways submit to him, and he will make your paths straight." (Proverbs 3:5-6/NIV)

Many decisions in life require healthy amounts of courage, humility, counsel, careful consideration and time. There is one decision, however, that *shouldn't* wait. My dad and the repentant thief waited until the very last moments of their lives.

Why wait when you can have a personal relationship with God, the assurance of eternal life in Heaven, and a more abundant life here on Earth? The choice is simple and clear. If you haven't already, avoid the need for a buzzer beater and make that life-changing choice. Ask Jesus into your heart today.

Everybody needs to make a decision.

Study Questions

1. Have you ever played in a game or watched a game where someone had to hit a last-second shot or make a last-minute play to come out with the win? Were you nervous? Excited? Fearful?

2. What are some big decisions you've faced recently? Did you find it easy or difficult to make those choices?

3. One of the thieves joined in with the crowd and mocked Jesus. The other recognized He was the Son of God. How often have you allowed the opinions of others to discourage you from making an important decision? Why do you think fear is such a powerful enemy of change?

4. What do you think are the most important ways you can weigh the costs of an important decision? How do things like wise counsel, measured judgment and prayerful consideration play a factor when you are making a decision?

5. My father made a decision to accept Christ in the last few hours of his life. Do you need to make that choice? Do you know someone else who needs to make that choice? If the answer for yourself is yes, consider praying the prayer found in the Afterword (Meet My Head Coach, pp. 243-244) and asking Jesus into your heart. If the answer for someone you know is yes, be courageous and unashamed to share the Good News of Jesus so they too might have eternal life.

Prayer

Lord, help me to make better decisions in my life. Give me the courage to overcome fear. Give me the humility to overcome pride. Give me the wisdom that is available through wise counsel, measured judgment and prayerful consideration. Most importantly, be the Lord of my life. I want to make the daily decision to serve You and help others know You too. Amen.

CHAPTER FIFTEEN

CENTER COURT
Everybody Needs A Timeout

"We need quiet time to examine our lives openly and honestly. Spending quiet time alone gives your mind an opportunity to renew itself and create order." – Susan L. Taylor

There's a reason basketball teams meet at center court. It's the same reason football teams meet at midfield and the same reason why baseball teams meet at the pitcher's mound. It's a place where teams can gather and become part of the inner circle. As the players and coaches gather in that circle, they can really start to feel the collective heartbeat that is so vital to team unity.

Throughout my coaching career, center court was significant on many occasions but perhaps none more so than my early days at St. John's. As I entered my first season there, I was excited about the talent I had inherited from departing head coach Fran Fraschilla. Just the thought of playing in the Big East and Madison Square Garden gave me goose bumps.

At the top of the list was sophomore All-American candidate Ron Artest, a highly recruited player out of New York City. I had seen him play many times when he was with the AAU program at Riverside Church. The first time I met Ron was in our first team meeting, the day I was hired. I quickly discovered Ron was like no other player I had ever coached.

During the hiring process, Ron showed great concern about who his next head coach was going to be. He was not happy with his lack of involvement in the process. Ron thought very highly of himself and wanted a coach who could help him get to the NBA. During that first meeting with the team, Ron didn't say much. In fact, he asked just one question.

"Coach," he said, "Do you *really* believe that we can win the national championship?"

I could tell from the tone in his voice that he had his doubts and wanted to see how I would respond. He was testing me.

"Ron," I said. "I need you to do a little homework on me. I need you to check my background and see where I've coached, whom I've coached and what I've done. I left a great job at George Washington to come to St. John's because I wanted the challenge of coaching in New York City. I came here to win, and I wouldn't be here if I didn't think we could win it all."

Tickets, Typewriters and Timeouts

Over the years, I've had some incredible relationships with players, but my relationship with Ron was all business. He didn't want a father figure or a friend. Ron just wanted a basketball coach, someone he respected, someone who could make him better.

Right away, I found out how hard he practiced and how driven and intense he was. Ron expected everyone to play at the same level and with the same intensity as he did. His expectations as a player were off the chart and his expectations of his teammates were equally high. Whether his teammate was a great talent or the last man on the team, Ron wanted that player to perform at his level, which was impossible.

Ron would go off on his teammates if they didn't do exactly what they were supposed to do. There were times when I doubted my ability to keep him in control, not just on the court during practice, but in certain settings away from the court as well. We might be having a team dinner, and everything would be going great. Ron would be nice and quiet and a very loving, wonderful person. Then all of the sudden, he would explode.

On at least two separate occasions, Ron requested several extra game tickets. There are strict rules and regulations about how many tickets you can get for the players, and sometimes we just didn't have enough, especially when we were playing in Madison Square

Garden. On those occasions when we weren't able to give Ron what he needed, he would get very emotional and storm out of the restaurant before the end of the pre-game meal. Fifteen minutes later, the quiet, calm Ron would return and life would go on as if nothing had happened.

Practice, however, was my biggest challenge. Could we get through an entire practice like a normal team, or would I have to deal with my star player's mood swings?

After a lot of prayer, I decided to appeal to Ron's spiritual side and involve the one person that I thought he would listen to. That was God Himself.

Any time Ron got out of control, I would call a timeout and huddle the team up at midcourt. Then, I would ask the team priest, Father Maher, to join us and lead us in prayer. Many times it was simply the Lord's Prayer and Ron was good to go. If a second timeout was necessary, we would repeat the process and finish the practice on a positive note.

However, during one of our Sunday night practices, things went terribly awry. It happened to be the night that my dear friend Bishop William DeVeaux, who was my pastor at Metropolitan A.M.E. Church in Washington D.C. stopped by to watch practice. Before we started, I introduced Bishop DeVeaux to the team and asked him to lead us in prayer. I just knew that this was going to be a great practice.

Things started out nicely. Then all of the sudden, Ron became agitated at one of his teammates and disrupted everything. I signaled a timeout and called the team, the priest and the Bishop to center court where Father Maher led us in the Lord's Prayer. We followed that with a brief water break and went back to work.

It wasn't long before something else irritated Ron and he blew up a second time. Like before, I blew my whistle and called for another team prayer. Under normal circumstances, I would have advocated for a more immediate form of discipline, but Ron was different and the timeout policy was in effect. Shortly thereafter, I had to call a third timeout. Just like baseball, three strikes and you're out.

This time I told the team to get some water and called Ron over to me.

"Ron, you're going to have to leave," I calmly told him.

Ron loved to practice and was shocked when I lowered my voice and asked him to leave. Taking gym time away from him was probably the worst thing in the world I could do to him, but it was the only thing that would get his attention and hopefully change his behavior. I'm sure Ron would rather I had shown anger towards him so he could blame me for his troubles.

"I'll see you tomorrow," I said.

With my bishop sitting on the bench, Ron proceeded to take the basketballs off the rack and heave them into the bleachers. Once the basketballs were gone, he tossed the ball rack for good measure before storming towards the exit. As practice came to a close, one of my managers informed me that Ron had trashed the locker room.

I decided to deal with Ron in the morning and said goodbye to Bishop DeVeaux before heading upstairs to my office. When I walked in, I immediately noticed that something was different. Legendary St. John's head coach Lou Carneseca's antique typewriter was not in its usual place on the table next to the secretary's desk. Thanks to Ron Artest, it had found a new home lodged in the wall that led into my office.

"Check underneath my car for a bomb," I kiddingly told my son.

Mike and I laughed and went home.

I didn't sleep very well that night in anticipation of my meeting with Ron the next morning. I had no idea what to expect. But when he arrived for our conversation, he was very calm and contrite. Ron apologized profusely for what he had done. I informed him we would have to deduct some money from his monthly stipend to pay for the damages and that he would be suspended from practice for three days.

Ron still had his challenges. There were some games when I would have to call a timeout just to calm him down, but because of his desire to win and perform well, and a big assist from prayer, we were usually able to get him back on track. Ron was the most important and versatile member of a team that came within three points of a Final Four appearance during the 1998-99 season.

That spring, he left school and entered the NBA draft, where the Indiana Pacers drafted him in the first round. At Indiana he was involved in the infamous "Malice At The Palace" melee where a brawl between the Pacers and the Detroit Pistons spilled into the crowd.

Eventually, Ron was diagnosed with some unspecified emotional conditions that many have speculated was bi-polar disorder. He began taking medication to help control his severe mood swings and in essence save his career. Ron also changed his name to Metta World Peace, a fitting decision based on his quirky personality, and he went on to win an NBA Championship with the 2010 Los Angeles Lakers.

Early in his career and long before his mental health issues were addressed, I routinely received phone calls from Indiana's management asking how I was able to handle Ron during his college playing days.

"I didn't handle him," I would always say. "God did."

Then I would tell them about the prayer meetings at center court. I don't know if they believed me, but it was certainly true. Prayer always had a way of calming Ron down.

The Great Getaway

In the book of Exodus, we read about the iconic Jewish leader Moses. He had already led the Israelites out of Egyptian captivity and was now doing his best to keep the increasingly disgruntled group from turning its back on God and completely falling apart.

On many occasions, Moses became frustrated and even belligerent with his own people. In order to keep his sanity, he often took timeouts, so to speak. He made a consistent effort to get away from the masses and spend time talking to God, reflecting on his past experiences, and meditating on what God had revealed to him.

These getaways often resulted in some very significant

moments. In Exodus 20, for example, God gave Moses the Ten Commandments during one of his getaways up into Mount Sinai. That instruction from God became the pillar of Judaic law and greatly influenced some of modern society's common moral principles.

We later read about an encounter Moses had with God during a 40-day timeout away from the people. In Exodus 34 and 35, God allowed Moses to catch a glimpse of His being. He then renewed His covenant, a divine agreement, between Himself and the Israelites. Even though Moses did not eat or drink during that time, he returned to the people refreshed and renewed. For many days after, Moses had to wear a veil over his face because God's glory shone so brightly from his skin. His quiet time with God had changed him physically, emotionally and spiritually.

Moses wasn't the only biblical figure to enjoy the benefits of getting away. Even Jesus needed a timeout. He often stole away from His disciples and the masses that were following Him, listening to His teachings and clamoring for a healing touch. In those times when the hysteria was reaching a fevered pitch Jesus would go to a quiet place, like out on a boat, out in the wilderness or sitting beneath an olive tree in a garden.

In fact, the Bible tells us that, "Jesus often withdrew to lonely places and prayed." (Luke 5:16/NIV)

Perhaps the most famous instance of Jesus seeking solitude occurred in the hours leading up to His crucifixion. After the Lord's Supper (Luke 22:14-20), He asked His disciples to accompany him to the Garden of Gethsemane. Although they were unable to stay awake, Jesus prayed late into the night as He agonized over what was about to happen.

"Father, if it is Your will, take this cup away from Me; nevertheless not my will, but Yours be done." (Luke 22:42)

Even as He agonized over the pain and suffering He was about to endure, it was that time of prayer and quiet time with God that gave Him the strength to face the unthinkable.

Everybody Needs A Timeout

Everybody needs a place where they can go for a timeout. If

you're a basketball coach, it might be center court. In your everyday life, it might be the living room couch, a bench at the neighborhood park, or your favorite spot at the beach.

Wherever it might be, taking a timeout is something everyone should do on a regular basis. Here are four ways you can start to implement timeouts or quiet times in your life:

1. Think before you speak: In general, we all have those moments where we can easily lose control of a difficult situation if we allow the first thoughts that come into our mind to turn into words or actions. Sometimes we need to simply take a momentary timeout just to allow ourselves to process what is going on and avoid saying or doing things we might regret.

"Do not be quick with your mouth, do not be hasty in your heart to utter anything before God. God is in heaven and you are on earth, so let your words be few." (Ecclesiastes 5:2/NIV)

2. Be consistent: Pick a day of the week, a time of the day and a particular place that works for you and allows you to get into a habitual routine. Then, be vigilant and don't allow hectic circumstances to dictate your ability to keep that consistent quiet time.

"I meditate on your precepts and consider your ways. I delight in your decrees; I will not neglect your word." (Psalm 119:15-16/NIV)

3. Be quiet: This might seem a little redundant, but sadly, we sometimes have a difficult time actually being *quiet* during quiet time. Certainly, a timeout is a great time to pray and share our thoughts with God. But at some point, it's important to stop and be silent. Use the time to read the Bible or another inspirational book. And then don't end your quiet time without reflecting on what you've read and listening for instruction and encouragement from the Holy Spirit.

4. Rest up: Timeouts aren't limited to brief interludes away from the craziness of life. In fact, there's nothing like a good night's sleep to allow your mind to rest and your body to recover from the stresses you may have faced throughout the day. When you are physically and mentally tired, it becomes more difficult to make good choices and avoid rash confrontations that only add to your troubles. Being well rested can help you think more clearly, react more succinctly, and proceed with greater efficiency when difficult decisions come your way. God set an example when He rested on the seventh day of Creation (Genesis 2:2) and has given us the gift of rest for our bodies and our minds.

"For anyone who enters God's rest also rests from their works, just as God did from His." (Hebrews 4:10/NIV)

"Be still, and know that I am God." (Psalm 46:10a/NIV)

5. Be encouraged: Things don't change overnight and one or two timeouts might not yield the immediate results you are looking for. Don't give up. Be encouraged that God *will* meet you in your quiet times and bring the refreshing peace and insightful wisdom you so desperately need.

"In all my prayers for all of you, I always pray with joy because of your partnership in the gospel from the first day until now, being confident of this, that he who began a good work in you will carry it on to completion until the day of Christ Jesus. (Philippians 1:4-6/NIV)

It isn't always easy, and our lives don't always allow us to have the perfect quiet time we need, but being intentional is the key to making the most of those timeouts that we take throughout the days and weeks of our lives. It is from those quiet times that we emerge refreshed, enlightened and strengthened to do the things for which we have been purposed.

Everybody needs a timeout.

Study Questions

1. What do you think about when you hear the word "timeout?"

2. Have you ever dealt with situations where you felt like you needed a timeout or simply needed to get away for a while? Were you you able to take a timeout? If so, how did getting away help the situation?

3. Of all the stories discussed in this chapter (Ron Artest, Moses and Jesus in the Garden), which one were you able to relate to the most? Explain.

4. Go back and look at the five items regarding how to implement timeouts in your life. Which of these things have you been successful at doing and how have they helped you?

5. Which of those five things has been difficult to implement and why? How do you think they might improve your life and make it easier to accomplish your goals?

6. What are some things you can start doing today that will allow you to take better advantage of this concept of timeouts or quiet times?

Prayer

Lord, slow me down. Reveal to me the importance of timeouts in my life. I want to hear from You. I desire Your wisdom. I want to receive Your peace and Your encouragement. Help me make a plan of action and give me the grace to stick with that plan. Rid my life of the distractions that might keep me from having regular quiet times with You. Amen.

CHAPTER SIXTEEN

THE COURAGE TO FORGIVE
Everybody Needs A Second Chance

"We must develop and maintain the capacity to forgive. He who is devoid of the power to forgive is devoid of the power to love." – *Martin Luther King, Jr.*

When I was a sophomore basketball player at Northeastern University, I made one of the biggest mistakes of my life. I quit the team. I thought I was better than I was and felt like head coach Dick Dukeshire should be giving me more playing time.

The truth was I didn't have a good grasp on the fundamentals of the game. I had talent, but my talent was more limited than I realized. While I was away from the team, I went to work for my brother Richard at his fish and chips restaurant, which was across the street from my house on River Street in Cambridge. With the help of my brother and the burn marks that I received frying seafood, it didn't take me long to realize that I had made a foolish decision.

At the conclusion of the basketball season, I apologized for my inappropriate behavior and begged Coach Dukeshire for the opportunity to rejoin the team. Coach Dukeshire could have written me off and decided I was too much trouble, but instead, he forgave me and graciously offered me a second chance.

That's when I realized that God had me right where He wanted me, and that was with a man who could prepare me for my calling as a basketball coach. I could now focus my attention on completing an undergraduate degree in physical education and a master's degree in education. My goal was to return to my high school alma mater and build a program that would prepare its players for success on and off the court.

Every night, before I fell asleep, I would write down the day's practice plan, the plays, the key teaching points, and the words Coach Dukeshire had used that day. I still have the blue binder notebook which I plan on sharing with my grandchildren when I talk to them about God's grace and second chances.

What if Coach Dukeshire didn't give me a second chance? Where would I be today? I'm glad I don't have to answer that question.

Four Powerful Letters

In my first year at St. John's, thanks to the recruiting efforts of the previous head coach Fran Fraschilla, I inherited a group of talented players, including a future NBA lottery pick named Ron Artest and a McDonald's All-American point guard named Erick Barkley.

Raised in Brooklyn, Erick went to Christ the King High School before attending prep school at Maine Central Institute under legendary coach Max Goode. Many coaches, myself included, ranked Erick as the #1 defensive backcourt player in the country. He was a tenacious defender who had the look of an assassin and struck fear into the heart of the opposing team's floor general. His goal was to control the game at both ends of the floor and help his team win. Most of the time, that's exactly what he did.

During that 1998-99 season, we went 28-9 and advanced to the NCAA Tournament's Elite Eight. In the regional final against fourth-ranked Ohio State, Erick was involved in a controversial play late in the game. With less than a minute remaining, Scoonie Penn stole the ball from Erick. It was obvious to everyone except the referees that Erick was fouled. That play ultimately allowed Ohio State to pull off a 77-74 victory and dashed our Final Four hopes. It was a tough ending to Erick's freshman year and his dream of winning a national championship.

With everyone returning except Ron Artest, our team was poised and confident that we could win the Big East and NCAA championships. However, before the start of the 1999-2000 season, the NCAA singled out several high profile players from across the country for investigation. The list included JaRon Rush (UCLA), Kareem Rush (Missouri), DerMarr Johnson (Cincinnati), Corey Maggette (Duke) and Erick Barkley.

The NCAA thought it could make a statement and bust the biggest AAU programs wide open if they could prove that Erick and the other players had received illegal gifts from their AAU teams. It was alleged that Erick had received his automobile from Ernie Lorche and the Riverside Hawks.

The assumption was that these players would only play one or two years before going to the pros and that they had no intention of earning a degree. Unfortunately, we will never know.

On numerous occasions, the NCAA sent investigators to St. John's and took Erick out of class and off the court. It was an incredibly stressful process that was ripe with intimidation and innuendo.

As the season progressed, the situation with Erick continued to deteriorate. On February 5, 2000, two hours before an afternoon game against Boston College, we got word that he was going to be suspended. The NCAA had determined that Erick received an extra benefit when he traded his 1996 Jeep Cherokee for an older but larger Chevrolet Suburban that one of his former youth league coaches owned.

It didn't matter that St. John's received no competitive advantage or that Erick's actions had no direct impact on his decision to play there. All that mattered was the NCAA's desire to indict the system. At the time, I did not have very much faith in the NCAA. I went off on the organization during the postgame interview.

Later in that season, while the team was getting dressed for a Big East game against Villanova in Madison Square Garden, we received a phone call notifying us that Erick was suspended again. I believe that the NCAA was trying to get him to quit, but somehow, the kid and the team got through it.

There was so much tension and fear that entire season. There was so much turmoil and uncertainty. On any given day, we could get a call and be notified that our starting point guard was not going to be eligible to play. We didn't just have to beat the other team. We had to beat the NCAA. It was us against them, and we were *not* going to let them beat us.

The fight with the NCAA made us stronger, and we were more determined than ever to beat our opponents. First and foremost, however, we wanted to beat the NCAA. We kept climbing in the Big East standings and in the national rankings. After our victory over Villanova in early February we continued to stay in contention for the conference title and a top 10 ranking. As the month came to a close, we prepared to play Syracuse, Duke, and Connecticut in an eight-day span. *Sports Illustrated* dubbed it "Hell Week." We won all three games, and for a short period of time Erick and his teammates didn't have to think about the NCAA.

As tough as it was for the team, I can't imagine what Erick was going through. Somehow, and mostly because of his upbringing in a tough environment, he survived. Thanks to the ominous cloud that hung over our heads, though, the team was on edge. Off the court, the players were uptight. An unusual amount of arguments and an occasional fistfight took place. On the court, however, the team was in harmony. On offense, all five guys ran the old Boston Celtics weave offense to perfection.

After a season-ending overtime loss at Miami, we ended up back in the Garden for the Big East conference tournament. We won our opening round game against Villanova and were then matched up once again with the Miami Hurricanes. It was a defensive struggle and we trailed by four points as the first half was coming to a close. During the last time out of the half, Erick got in his senior teammate Bootsy Thornton's face and challenged him to play better defense.

As I took the walk down the hall and approached the locker room, I noticed the referees were standing outside the door. They stood there frozen with nervous looks on their faces.

I opened the door to find Erick and Bootsy brawling in the middle of the Knicks' locker room. Forget about strategy. Forget about Miami. I had to break up a fight between my starting point guard and leading scorer.

Moving as quickly as I could, I threw my arms around Erick and carried him over to the trainer's table. In the process, my gold chain cut his arm. When he saw the blood, he panicked. It took another five minutes to calm Erick down, and now it was time to leave for the second half. I turned to my assistants and told them to take the players back to the court.

"I quit!" Erick said, as he started to take off his uniform.

After catching my breath, I sat down next to Erick and did my best to settle him down.

"We have come this far together," I said. "We've gone through all this stuff and I've been with you every step of the way. I've fought you."

But Erick wasn't interested in my words of encouragement. He just wanted someone to lash out against, and I was the only person available.

"You cut me!" Erick angrily said. "I'm gonna have my boys get you after the game."

"That's okay," I calmly replied. "Have them get me after we win."

Erick didn't respond, but instead put his jersey back on and headed out to the court.

The second half was already underway when the two of us returned to the bench. You could hear a buzz in the stands. No one, including our players, knew what was going on. I put Erick back into the game as soon as possible. We fought hard and ended up winning a nail biter, 58-57. Anthony Glover and Lavar Postell hit four consecutive free throws to seal the victory. Erick finished with seven points and five assists. Four of those passes were to his halftime boxing opponent, Bootsy Thornton.

At 12:30 a.m., the press conference ended. As we were making our way to the bus, Erick approached me.

"I'm taking a leave of absence," he said.

After the 10-minute ride back to the hotel, I met up with my family and my assistant coaches to get something to eat. It was 1 a.m., when I looked up and saw Erick leaving the hotel with a couple of his friends.

Erick went back to Brooklyn and I was left with a bizarre situation to manage. We had scheduled a practice at MSG for 1 p.m. the next afternoon, but there was no way I was going to take the players into the media circus that would be waiting for us. Instead, we took the 30-minute bus ride to Alumni Hall on our campus in Queens.

Just before we left the hotel, Erick's mother called to tell me that her son had been crying all night. He was terribly sorry and wanted to rejoin the team. I told her to have Erick meet us in the locker room.

By then, practice was going to be a useless proposition. We had just played the night before, and our next game was going to be our third game that year against UConn. We still had to figure out what to do about Erick. I knew we had to do something.

Erick asked if he could speak to the team. He immediately apologized and told his teammates he was terribly sorry about what he had done. He told them how much he wanted to play and help them win the championship. As he was speaking, I looked down at my wrist and noticed the red cloth bracelet I was wearing. On it was four simple, but powerful letters: W.W.J.D. At the time, "What Would Jesus Do," had become an oft-used phrase within the Christian community. It also represented a movement that pervaded popular culture.

Ironically, it was Erick who had given me the bracelet a few weeks earlier, along with a black one with the same threaded inscription. For what he had gone through, I really wanted him to play. I wanted him to end the season on the court with the team.

So after Erick sat down, I walked to the blackboard and wrote the letters "W.W.J.D."

"W.W.J.D." I said to the team. "What would Jesus do?"

Then, I went around the room and asked the guys that question individually. Sure enough, every one of them felt like Jesus would forgive Erick and give him another chance.

"You know what?" I added. "I'm not arguing with Jesus. Get dressed! Let's go eat."

We went to Dante's Italian restaurant for our customary pregame meal and then took a bus ride to the Garden. When we arrived, there were cameras and reporters everywhere.

They all wanted to know what was going on with Erick. Was he going to play? Everyone's response was the same.

"We came to play and win the Big East Championship."

That night, it was like nothing had happened. We played inspired team basketball and were in total control at both ends of the court. After an 80-70 victory, and especially after all the team had endured, it was quite rewarding to cut down the nets. Bootsy Thornton was named tournament MVP, while Erick Barkley and Lavar Postell were named to the All-Tournament Team. A day later, we would be rewarded with a #2 seed in the NCAA Tournament.

It would have been easy to write Erick off. But when I saw him speaking to his teammates in that locker room, I realized that he was just a scared kid who had been beaten down by the NCAA and the rigors of a long season. When I looked down and saw those initials on my bracelet, I was reminded that he deserved a second chance, just like the one that Coach Dukeshire gave me, and just like the second chance that Jesus gives to all of us.

The Prodigal Son

In a way, those stories are both reminiscent of the biblical parable of the prodigal son Jesus shared with His followers (Luke 15:11-32/NIV). Here's an abridged version:

A man had two sons. The younger son wanted his share of the family estate even though it was not yet time for him to receive his inheritance. The father agreed and gave the son what he was due. Shortly thereafter, the son took all of his possessions and traveled to a far away country. Before long, he had squandered all of his wealth.

About that time, there was a famine in the land. The young man became desperate for food and shelter. He took a job feeding a farmer's pigs and was so hungry that he craved the slop he was feeding the animals.

With starvation and death staring him down, he finally realized he had no other choice but to go home and beg for his father to hire him as a servant. As he neared his home, his father was waiting in the distance. The father ran to his son, "threw his arms around him and kissed him." (v. 20)

"Father, I have sinned against heaven and against you. I am no longer worthy to be called your son." (v. 21)

The father rejected that notion. He called his servants to bring his son the best robe for him to wear. He also gave him a ring and some sandals for his feet. The father then threw a party in his son's honor. (vv. 22-24)

Interestingly, Jesus gives us a glimpse of the other side of forgiveness from the perspective of the older brother. When he saw all the attention his recently returned brother was getting, he became angry and refused to join the rest of the family for the welcome back party (v. 28). He couldn't believe his father would so easily embrace a son who had carelessly squandered his inheritance.

There was certainly an element of jealousy at play and the absence of true, forgiving love. Jesus doesn't tell us what happens next, but the older brother appeared to be opening the door to that dangerous heart condition known as bitterness.

It takes courage to forgive, even when the person who needs forgiveness is someone close to you. In my story with Coach Dukeshire, what I had done was immature and disrespectful, but quitting the team wasn't terribly egregious. Still, my coach was not obligated to let me back on the team. I'm thankful he had it in his heart to give me that second chance.

The same was true with Erick Barkley. His act of walking away from the team was also wrong and selfish, but thanks to the brotherhood and familial love in the St. John's locker room, he was likewise welcomed back into the fold.

In the story of the prodigal son, the father's love for his youngest child overcame the presence of any anger or disappointment. That's what true love looks like. Love brings forth courage. Courage brings forth forgiveness. And forgiveness brings forth second chances.

Everybody Needs A Second Chance

Forgiveness isn't always easy. In fact, forgiveness can be one of the single most difficult acts for us to carry out. When we fail to forgive others, we might think it's somehow hurting the other person, but it's actually hurting us. In the end, forgiveness is liberating and healthy for the soul.

Here are three simple ways we can all do a better job forgiving others and opening the door to the gift of second chances:

1. Show mercy: Often times when we are hurt, our first gut reaction is to show disapproval, disappointment and even anger. Those emotions and actions are hard to take back. Instead, we need to train ourselves to show kindness and mercy to those who hurt us or let us down.

"My dear brothers and sisters, take note of this: Everyone should be quick to listen, slow to speak and slow to become angry." (James 1:19/NIV)

2. See the big picture: Too often, we try to play God and make decisions about who has a chance to make it and who doesn't. In some situations, it might seem easier to write someone off as a lost cause. Not forgiving them and not giving them a second chance is much more convenient when we don't recognize the potential and purpose God has placed in their life. It also shows a lack of faith in God's ability to work miracles and turn something around for His glory.

"In (Christ) we were also chosen, having been predestined according to the plan of Him who works out everything in conformity with the purpose of His will, in order that we, who were the first to put our hope in Christ, might be for the praise of his glory." (Ephesians 1:11-12/NIV)

3. Let it go: At the risk of invoking a popular Disney theme song and sounding terribly cliché at the same time, there is some real power to letting go of any hurt or bitterness that can so easily hang around. Letting go of those toxic thoughts and emotions seals the act of forgiveness. It allows everyone involved to move forward.

"Get rid of all bitterness, rage, anger, harsh words, and slander, as well as all types of evil behavior. Instead, be kind to each other, tenderhearted, forgiving one another, just as God through Christ has forgiven you." (Ephesians 4:31-32/NLT)

And guess what? These principles also apply when the person you need to forgive is *yourself.* When you make a mistake, give yourself a break. Don't be so hard on yourself. Know that God is *still* working on you and that He *still* has a plan for your life. And then let go of the past and rid yourself of the weight of guilt and shame.

"Forgetting the past and looking to what lies ahead, I press on to reach the end of the race and receive the heavenly prize for which God, through Christ Jesus, is calling us." (Philippians 3:13b-14)

Ultimately, we really can't know true forgiveness until we know true love. And that's the kind of love that only comes from a God who doesn't just give us the ability to love but *is* love (1 John 4:8). From the beginning of time until today, God has been about the business of forgiveness and second chances, both of which are rooted in His love.

Everybody needs a second chance.

Study Questions

1. Think of a time you were faced with the choice to forgive or not forgive someone for something they did to you. What choice did you make and how did that choice impact your immediate future?

2. Think of a time when you needed someone to forgive you. What did they choose to do and how did their choice affect you?

3. Of the three stories discussed in this chapter (Coach Dukeshire, Erick Barkley and the prodigal son), with which could you most closely relate? Explain.

4. Why is it so hard for us to forgive others?

5. Of the three keys to forgiveness given, which ones have you struggled to follow through with in your life? Why so and how has it affected you and your relationships with others?

6. Of the three keys to forgiveness given, which ones have been easier to apply to your life? What has that done for you and for your relationships with others?

Prayer

Lord, thank You for forgiving me. Thank You for the gift of second chances. Fill me with Your perfect love so I might have the courage to forgive others when they hurt me. Give me the strength to forgive myself when I make mistakes and disappoint others. Amen.

CHAPTER SEVENTEEN

LENNY, LeBRON AND THE REAL MJ
Everybody Needs A Reality Check

"Do not think of yourself more highly than you ought, but rather think of yourself with sober judgment, in accordance with the faith God has distributed to each of you." – Apostle Paul (Romans 12:3/NIV)

It's a little known fact that I was once offered the head coaching job with the Washington Wizards. It was early 2000, and Michael Jordan had just become part owner and president of basketball operations.

At the time, I was the head coach at St. John's University and wasn't sure if I wanted to be an NBA coach, but it was an offer that was certainly worth entertaining. It got so serious that Michael came to New York as my special guest at the Metropolitan Club, where we were having an annual fundraiser. The next day he came to my house to talk about the job. The meeting lasted about three hours, and it went well.

Less than a week later, my agent Rob Ades went to meet with Michael to hammer out the final details. After a third meeting, Rob called to tell me they could not come to terms, and there would be no deal. He then made me laugh when he told me how the meeting ended. It was a story I would hear countless times. Rob told me that as he headed toward the door, Michael took down a Louisville Slugger that was mounted on his office wall.

"Aha!" Rob exclaimed. "Now I know why you didn't make it to the majors! You couldn't hit a damn thing with that bat!"

And then, Rob ran out the door as fast as he could.

Needless to say, the negotiations were officially over. The Wizards moved on and hired Leonard Hamilton the very next day.

What no one knew at the time was the fact that Michael was on the verge of a return to the basketball court. I honestly can't imagine trying to coach him during his comeback.

Even if I had taken the job, who knows what else might have happened? Many NBA coaches sacrifice their health and family relationships because of the lifestyle and demands of the position. Yes, I would have put quite a few extra dollars in my pocket, but I might have given up those things that meant the most.

That was one reality check I thankfully was able to avoid.

When The Greatest Wasn't Good Enough

My encounter with Michael Jordan back in 2000 wasn't the first. In fact, by then, I had developed a unique relationship with the iconic NBA legend.

It all started back in 1981. Because of my success at Cambridge Rindge and Latin High School where I happened to coach Patrick Ewing, the #1 player in the country, I had been invited to coach the East squad in the McDonald's All-American Game. Patrick had already played in two of the three major national events and was not eligible to play in a third, but he was allowed to travel with me to Wichita, Kansas.

Outside of Patrick, I had no idea who any of the players on either team would be. The first time I met Michael Jordan was the first time I met my East squad. At that point, he was just another talented high school basketball player. That was the purity of the game back then. There was no Twitter and no Facebook; it was before the Internet had become a household commodity.

I only coached Michael for a week, but it was a life-changing experience. He was an incredible player. He had such great work ethic and was fundamentally sound. Michael also had great passion and drive. There wasn't anything he couldn't do. Whatever Michael did, he tried to do it with everything he had. It didn't matter if it was the sprints we ran, he wanted to be the best and finish first.

Whenever I called the team to huddle up, Michael was the first to arrive so he could be front and center. He was all eyes and all ears. Michael didn't act like he was this great player. He looked me squarely in the eye and then went out and did whatever I asked him to do.

Michael was also generous with his time. He spent a lot of time with my son Mike who was my 12-year old assistant coach. In the team picture, you can see them standing next to each other. Michael also shared a story with my son that would become much more significant a few years down the road.

When Michael Jordan was a sophomore in high school, he did not make the varsity basketball team at Emsley A. Laney High School in Wilmington, North Carolina. He was only 5-11 at the time and considered too short and not good enough to play at that level. Michael shared with my son how his parents told him he was going to have to work harder and practice more. Michael would ask the custodian to let him into the gym at night so he could practice on his own. His tireless efforts and a four-inch growth spurt helped him make the cut the following year. Eventually, he became the star of the team. As a senior, he earned All-American status and finished second behind his college roommate Buzz Peterson for North Carolina's coveted Mr. Basketball award.

The rest is history.

I couldn't wait to get back to tell my Cambridge players about our 96-95 victory and how a kid named Michael Jordan scored our last four baskets, including the game-winning jump shot with three seconds left in the game. Just as importantly, I shared with them how Michael finished first in every race we had and how he was the only player I had ever coached who worked as hard as Patrick. I finished by telling the story that Michael told my son about how he dealt with being cut as a high school sophomore. His story was a great inspiration not only to my son but also to our upcoming players like Rumeal Robinson, who would later win a national championship at Michigan.

Along with Patrick, I knew Michael was going to be one of the next great NBA players. That next year, my assistant coach Al

Coccoluto joined my wife and me at the Final Four in New Orleans where we watched Patrick and Michael face off in the national championship game between Georgetown and North Carolina. During the closing seconds of the game, I leaned over to Al and said, "Georgetown better keep the ball out of Jordan's hands."

Sure enough, Hoyas guard Freddie Brown made the infamous bad pass right to North Carolina forward James Worthy who passed the ball to Michael Jordan. From the left baseline, Michael hit the game winning shot to give the Tar Heels the title. It was heartbreaking because we were there rooting for Patrick, but it was incredible to watch Michael's performance.

A few years later, when I was coaching at George Washington University, my wife and I often traveled to Nike sponsored trips along with other coaches like Mike Krzyzewski, Lute Olsen, P.J. Carlesimo, Jim Boeheim and Bill Frieder, as well as some elite NBA players like Jordan, Charles Barkley and David Robinson. They had some serious poker games on those trips that were usually out of my league, but I enjoyed watching from the side.

"Hey, it's the *real* MJ!" Michael would say when I walked into the room. "Come over and check us out!"

There's really no disputing the identity of the *real* MJ. Michael Jordan became known as such because of a reality check he took to heart and used as the motivation to go from, "not good enough" to "the greatest."

When King James Ruled

There was a time when a high school basketball player named Lenny Cooke was the king of New York. It didn't matter if it was the playground, the rec league or an AAU tournament, when Lenny showed up, crowds of people followed him to see what the kid was going to do. On the basketball court, Lenny was a legend.

Lenny came from a broken home in Brooklyn but lived with a wealthy woman named Debbie Bortner in Old Tapan, New Jersey, where he attended Northern Valley Regional High School.

In 2002, Sonny Vaccaro organized his annual Adidas All-American Camp at Farleigh Dickinson University in Teaneck, New Jersey. The event brought in the best prep players from across the country including future NBA athletes Joakim Noah and Sebastian Telfair, but there was no question that the headliners were Lenny Cooke and LeBron James, a rising star from Akron, Ohio.

Thousands of fans showed up to watch the games. I was one of numerous head coaches there to not just scout players but enjoy the spectacle. It was almost common knowledge that Lenny was going to play for me at St. John's if he didn't go pro. The kid could do it all.

But something happened at the camp that changed everything.

The entire event was building up to the matchup between Lenny and LeBron. Everything in New York is the biggest and the best, and Lenny was considered the biggest and the best on the court. He represented New York. That night was like an Ali-Frazier fight. The tension was palatable. The excitement level was off the charts. It was electric.

Early on, the matchup was fairly even, but as the game wore on, LeBron started to dominate. He made move after move, dunk after dunk. LeBron basically sat Lenny down and destroyed his team. More significantly, Lenny's ego was severely damaged. I don't think he ever recovered from that. His reputation as New York's finest suddenly disappeared. A lot of the people who were patting him on the back and telling him how great he was just went away. LeBron, later dubbed "King James," dethroned the king of New York.

Lenny was crushed. He was never the same. I saw him play a few more times during the high school season, but it was never against the highest level of competition. Lenny's encounter with LeBron should have been a reality check. He should have realized that he wasn't ready to play in the NBA. But because of stubbornness, too much pride and a lot of bad advice, Lenny declared for the 2002 NBA Draft.

It went downhill from there.

Lenny went unselected and didn't receive any offers to sign as a free agent. He spent the next five years bouncing around various semi-pro leagues and briefly played in China before an Achilles' tendon injury ended his career. His was a sad story about a kid who believed the hype. New York can do that to you. So can pride.

I can personally relate to what Lenny experienced. I often talk about how easy it is to get caught up in the lights of New York, to believe the hype and let one's pride get in the way.

Unfortunately, Lenny didn't have people telling him that he needed to go to college where he could develop his basketball skills, earn a degree and prepare for life after basketball. Instead of allowing his reality check to help him make a better decision, Lenny chose to ignore the signs that were so obvious to everyone else.

In December 2013, my wife and I sat in our family room and watched the documentary *Lenny Cooke* on Showtime. Today, Lenny is traveling around the country sharing his story with as many kids as possible so they won't make the same mistakes he made.

Everybody Needs A Reality Check

The Apostle Paul is one of the most famous New Testament figures. He has been lauded for his many contributions to biblical text, including letters to the churches in Rome, Corinth, Galatia, Phillipi, Ephesus, Colossae, and Thessalonica, as well as personal letters to Timothy and Philemon.

Paul wasn't always an inspirational evangelist to the Early Church. In fact, he was formerly known as Saul, an infamously tyrannical crusader against the burgeoning Christian movement. It took a harsh reality check from God Himself to force Saul to make a life-changing decision.

One day, while traveling on the road to Damascus, God struck Saul down with a flashing light. Then came these words from the skies:

"Saul, Saul, why do you persecute me?"

"Who are you, Lord?" Saul asked.

"I am Jesus, whom you are persecuting," he replied. "Now get up and go into the city, and you will be told what you must do." (Acts 9:3-6/NIV)

The encounter left Saul blind. His men helped bring him to Damascus, where a man named Ananias prayed for Saul. After his eyesight was restored, he was baptized and eventually transformed into a powerful man of God.

Perhaps that's why Paul, taking on the Latin version of his name, would later write these words:

"For by the grace given me I say to every one of you: Do not think of yourself more highly than you ought, but rather think of yourself with sober judgment, in accordance with the faith God has distributed to each of you." (Romans 12:3/NIV)

Paul had done great things, but he had also failed greatly. He understood better than anyone the importance of having an accurate self-assessment. Paul knew he wasn't as great as some thought. But he also knew he wasn't as worthless as his past might have suggested.

Michael Jordan took his reality check and used it to work harder and become the greatest NBA player of all time. The Apostle Paul wisely heeded his reality check and became a hero of the Christian faith. On the other hand, Lenny Cooke ignored his reality check and made some poor decisions that shortened his promising basketball career. Maybe Lenny's real journey is just beginning, though.

We all have reality checks. Sometimes we have more than one. The important thing is what we do with those moments when we are presented with the decision. Here are four ways we can make the most of our reality checks:

1. Don't believe the hype: It's easy to get puffed up amid success. Many times, pride is what brings on a reality check in the first place. If we avoid this common trap, we might just avoid some serious trouble.

"Pride comes before destruction, and an arrogant spirit before a fall." (Proverbs 16:18/HCSB)

2. Drown out the noise: When we do get that reality check, there are often many voices that start to make their presence known.

Sometimes it can be people in our lives telling us how badly we messed up, but most of the time it's simply that internal voice that silently tries to remind us of our mistakes or seeks to make us feel worthless and incapable of overcoming our adverse situation. Don't listen. These are nothing but lies from the enemy of our souls.

"Do not pay attention to every word people say." (Ecclesiastes 7:21a/NIV)

3. Stay positive: Even in the toughest times, we can stave off negative outside influences through positive reinforcement. The best place to find this is in friends and family members who believe in you and especially in the unchangeable Word of God. The biggest battle we will ever face is in our own minds. Staying positive is one strategic move that will help you win the war.

"Finally, brothers and sisters, whatever is true, whatever is noble, whatever is right, whatever is pure, whatever is lovely, whatever is admirable–if anything is excellent or praiseworthy–think about such things." (Philippians 4:8/NIV)

4. Know the truth about you: Instead of listening to the negative noise that will assuredly follow a reality check, we must remind ourselves of who we really are. We are loved. We have a purpose. We have value in God's eyes. We can overcome our challenges because of His strength inside of us.

"You, dear children, are from God and have overcome them, because the one who is in you is greater than the one who is in the world." (1 John 4:4/NIV)

It's not a matter of if reality checks will happen. It's a matter of when. They are never pleasant at the time, but if we allow them to, they will always bring clarity to our lives and help set us on the perfect path our Creator has laid out for us.

Everybody needs a reality check.

Study Questions

1. What is the most significant reality check you have ever received? What was your initial reaction? How did that reality check change your life?

2. Which of the three reality checks discussed (Michael Jordan, Lenny Cooke, Apostle Paul) most resonated with you and what you've experienced in your life? Explain.

3. What do you think is the source of reality checks? Do you think they always have a purpose? Explain.

4. Why do you think pride plays such a significant role in reality checks and how we respond to them?

5. Of the four keys to dealing with reality checks listed, which ones have you struggled with the most? What about that concept (or concepts) has been difficult for you to accept or implement?

6. If you are currently feeling the effects of a reality check, what are some things you can do today that will help you make the best of the situation? If you aren't currently dealing with a reality check, how do you think you might avoid one or better deal with the next one that comes your way?

Prayer

Lord, thank You for the reality checks that have come my way. Even though they can be difficult to go through, I know that You are using these situations to draw me closer and to move me in the right direction. Break me of my pride so that I will not resist Your correction. I want to fulfill the purpose You have placed in my life. Amen.

CHAPTER EIGHTEEN

RAZOR KRZYZEWSKI
Everybody Needs Respect

"I'm not concerned with your liking or disliking me. All I ask is that you respect me as a human being." – Jackie Robinson

Mike Krzyzewski is one of the greatest college basketball coaches of all-time. He has won over 1,000 games (the most of any NCAA Division 1 coach), five NCAA Championships, 13 ACC Tournament Championships, and four Olympic gold medals, two as the head coach and two as an assistant.

Coach K is also one of my dearest coaching friends. During the 1997-98 season, he served as the vice president of the National Association of Basketball Coaches (NABC) during my tenure as president. When my one-year term was over, I was honored to pass him the gavel at the Final Four. Over a 10 year period, we spent a lot of time together in committee meetings and gained a great deal of respect for one another.

"I need to give you a nickname," I once told him. "I hereby give you the nickname Razor Krzyzewski!"

"What do you mean by Razor?" he quizzically asked.

"No one realizes they've been cut by a razor until they can see the blood coming through their shirt," I explained. "You have such a great way of using words. You can cut a person up without them even knowing it."

That was certainly the truth. Coach K could slice through the heart of the matter with great efficiency. To this day, I still call him Razor.

Taking The Edge Off

To my surprise, Coach K didn't always live up to the moniker I gave him. In fact, on two separate occasions he showed a softer side to his competitive nature. Both instances were based solely on his respect for me and the game he loved.

It all started on January 24, 1999. That was the first meeting between one of my St. John's teams and one of Coach K's Duke teams. We were ranked #8 in the country and Duke was ranked #2. It was an incredible game in which we fought back from three double-digit deficits to force overtime. Ultimately, Duke won the game 92-88, but the mutual respect between Coach K and I only grew stronger. Afterward, we decided it should become an annual game.

The next year, our team was playing well late in the season, but anxiously dealing with the NCAA's investigation of our point guard, Erick Barkley. In an eight-day stretch that Sports Illustrated dubbed "Hell Week," we defeated Syracuse on the road, 76-75, Connecticut at home, 79-64, and then headed to Duke for a non-conference contest. Going into the game, the #2-ranked Blue Devils had a 64-game home winning streak against non-conference opponents. Even though we had yet to lose in the month of February, most prognosticators didn't give us much of a chance to pull off the upset.

To add to the pressure, Duke's student fans are exceptional at getting under the opposing team's skin with unique chants and very personal material. Famously known as "The Cameron Crazies," the fans did their homework and prepared all kinds of chants they planned to use regarding Erick.

But the night before the game, Coach K spoke to the students at a pep rally and asked them to be classy and not go after Erick. Coach K knew that Erick was already under enough attack from the NCAA. He essentially took a real weapon out of the students' hands. Coach K didn't want them to do something at the emotional expense of another human being, a young man who was playing the game he loved.

On February 26, 2000, our team stepped into the lion's den. The game was the CBS national game of the week. Even though it was late winter, it was 80 degrees outside and felt like 100 degrees inside Cameron Indoor Stadium. It was an incredible game that went back and forth and featured some incredible young talent. Duke had two exceptional freshmen, Jay Williams and Shane Battier, and several other future NBA stars like Carlos Boozer and Corey Maggette.

The previous year, Bootsy Thornton had scored 40 points in our loss against the Blue Devils. He came up big in this game as well. Bootsy had 22 points, 11 rebounds and six assists, but no play was more important than an 18-foot jumper that gave us the lead with 13 seconds remaining. After a Duke timeout, Chris Carrawell missed a 15-foot shot that bounded off the rim as time expired.

We won the game 83-82 and completed one of the most successful weeks in college basketball history.

The Duke victory was one of the most significant wins during my time at St. John's. ESPN extensively covered the game throughout the rest of the day, but there was a big part of the story that everyone missed. Had Coach K allowed his students to taunt Erick Barkley, it might have been a very different outcome. The chants could have unnerved him and things could have gotten really ugly. Instead, Erick played well. The crowd was almost *too* respectful.

The following season, Duke started a new streak. Heading into the 2015-16 season, Duke maintained an NCAA record of 117 non-conference home wins.

One of the things I admire most about Coach K is how he can totally focus on a game and throw personal relationships out the window. Yet, he didn't do that with me. I don't think he would ever admit it, but I believe that's part of the reason we beat Duke back in 2000. Coach K had too much love and respect for me and for my team.

Calming The Crazies

Four seasons later, Coach K had another opportunity to show respect and an uncanny sense of decorum. This time, the situation was even more personal. After winning the National Invitational Tournament (NIT) the year before, we had started the 2003-04 season with a disappointing 1-3 record. There was a player on the team who wasn't happy with his playing time and his girlfriend instigated a chant from the student section.

"Fi-re Jar-vis! Fi-re Jar-vis!"

On December 6, 2003, we returned to Duke where we faced a talented Blue Devils squad, led by future NBA star J.J. Redick, *and* the rowdy student section. Duke took a 20-point lead late into the game. That's when the chants started. True to form, the Cameron Crazies had done their homework.

"Fi-re Jar-vis!" they shouted in unison. "Fi-re Jar-vis!"

During the next timeout, Coach K didn't huddle up with players. Instead, he walked over to the scorer's table and grabbed the microphone.

"We will have *none* of that!" he barked with authority.

And guess what? The chant ended.

We lost 79-58. Not so ironically, I was fired following our next game, less than two weeks before Christmas. Because of the negative things that were happening in my life at the time, I don't think I fully appreciated what Coach K had done until later. Talk about class. He knew what Connie and I were going through. He also knew that I was every bit as good of a coach as I was when we beat Duke back in 2000. Coach K wasn't going to let his fans do that to me. His respect for me, my players, and for the game he loved was too strong.

All Hail The King

Showing respect for a friend is not generally that difficult a task, even in situations where it might cost something like a basketball game. But showing respect for an enemy is a completely different proposition. We find such an example in the Old Testament story of David and King Saul.

David and Saul weren't always enemies. In fact, when David was still young, he played music for Saul to help relieve him from spiritual oppression (1 Samuel 16). And of course, David went on to single-handedly defeat the Philistine giant called Goliath and lead the Israelite army to victory. (1 Samuel 17)

Not long after that iconic battle, Saul became jealous of David. That jealousy turned to fear. Saul was paranoid that David would overthrow his kingdom. So Saul decided to rid himself of the problem (1 Samuel 18).

He first tried to command his son Jonathan to kill David, but they were close friends and Jonathan refused to comply with his father's wishes. And then, on two separate occasions, Saul took matters into his own hands and tried to take David out of the picture but failed (1 Samuel 19).

David escaped Jerusalem and maneuvered throughout the region—into the wilderness, the hills, and the caves—to avoid Saul's murderous plot. And when David had the chance to kill Saul, not once, but twice, he spared the king's life out of respect for his authority.

"You are more righteous than I," King Saul said to David. "You have treated me well, but I have treated you badly…May the Lord reward you well for the way you treated me today" (1 Samuel 26:17, 19/NIV).

David's show of respect eventually helped Saul see the error of his ways. Unfortunately, it was too late to save his life. As Samuel had already prophesied, Saul and his three sons were killed in battle as punishment for his prior disobedience towards God (1 Samuel 30) and David was anointed as King of Judah (2 Samuel 3).

Things didn't end well for Saul. His inability to honor and respect David as God's anointed warrior was ultimately his undoing. But because David respected the king's authority, he was able to fulfill his destiny and assume leadership with a clear conscience.

Everybody Needs Respect

Everybody doesn't always deserve respect, at least not by man's standards. But the Bible tells us we should always strive to give respect and honor to each other as fellow human beings.

Coach K showed me respect even though it took away a competitive advantage that might have helped him win a basketball game. David showed respect for Saul even though the king was trying to kill him. Respect isn't always an easy thing to give. It can often be a humbling experience. This can be true when we are in a difficult family situation, when we disagree with someone in governmental authority over us, or when someone has hurt us.

Let's take a look at what the Bible has to say about the tricky topic of respect and to whom we are called to show honor:

1. Respect yourself: It's true. We know ourselves better than anyone else. And because we are human and make mistakes, sometimes our self-respect can be diminished. But respect for others starts with having respect for ourselves based on the fact that God loves us, even when we don't feel like we deserve it.

"Do you not know that your bodies are temples of the Holy Spirit, who is in you, whom you have received from God? You are not your own; you were bought at a price. Therefore honor God with your bodies." (1 Corinthians 6:19-20/NIV)

2. Respect your family: My siblings and I didn't have the world's greatest dad, but my mom always taught us to respect him and love him because he was our father. It doesn't matter if your parents or your spouse or your siblings or your extended family members have let you down, show them honor and respect, and they will be better for it.

"Children, obey your parents in the Lord, for this is right. Honor your father and mother—which is the first commandment with a promise—so that it may go well with you and that you may enjoy long life on the earth. Fathers, do not exasperate your children; instead, bring them up in the training and instruction of the Lord." (Ephesians 6:1-4/NIV) .

3. Respect your fellow man: All human beings are created in God's image. That fact alone serves as the impetus for respecting those with whom we come into contact on a daily basis. People don't always treat each other nicely, but giving respect to acquaintances or total strangers is what the Bible instructs us to do, and that show of respect just might melt someone's heart and help he or she experience God's love.

"Love the Lord your God with all your heart and with all your soul and with all your mind. This is the first and greatest commandment. And the second is like it: Love your neighbor as yourself. All the Law and the Prophets hang on these two commandments." (Matthew 22:36-40/NIV)

4. Respect your fellow believers: Churches can be a lot like families. They love each other deeply but at the same time are prone to argue, bicker and fight. When that happens, there's a very real temptation to lose respect for those with whom we find ourselves at odds. But the Bible is clear. We must do everything in our power to maintain civility within the Body of Christ so the world will see God's love working through us.

"Be devoted to one another in love. Honor one another above yourselves." (Romans 12:10/NIV)

5. Respect your enemies: This might be one of the toughest commandments in the Bible. Respecting those who have hurt you doesn't mean being okay with what they have done. It simply means showing love and forgiveness in spite of that pain. There's something powerful about honoring those who would seek to destroy us. It is often that compassionate display that turns hearts back to God.

"You have heard that it was said, 'Love your neighbor and hate your enemy.' But I tell you, love your enemies and pray for those who persecute you." (Matthew 5:43-44/NIV)

6. Respect your authorities: Respecting someone doesn't necessarily mean always agreeing with them. This is certainly the case when it comes to those who have leadership over us at work, at church, or (this is the tough one for many of us) in government. Does this mean we must comply with authorities who ask us to do things that compromise our values or our commitment to God? Absolutely not. God is the authority above all authorities, but we should still maintain respect for those who preside over us and pray for the Spirit to lead them in everything they do.

"Show proper respect to everyone, love the family of believers, fear God, honor the emperor." (1 Peter 2:17/NIV)

7. Respect your Creator: There is no way we can truly show respect to anyone else (ourselves included) if we don't first respect God, but it's not just about admiring God or being okay with God's existence. It's deeper than that. It's about honoring and revering God, recognizing Him as the ultimate authority figure in our lives. As we learn to put God first, He then gives us the ability to love and respect others no matter how difficult that might seem.

"Therefore, since we are receiving a kingdom which cannot be shaken, let us have grace, by which we may serve God acceptably with reverence and godly fear. For our God *is* a consuming fire. (Hebrews 12:28-29/NIV)

Respect is born out of love and humility. Once we have a greater understanding of God's love for us and how His Son Jesus humbled Himself as the ultimate example of that love, we can then start to show respect for ourselves, our friends, our family members, those within the Body of Christ and even those we disagree with or consider our enemies.

Everybody needs respect.

Study Questions

1. What does the word "respect" mean to you? What are some ways we can show respect for others?

2. In the two stories about St. John's and Duke, what would you have done if you had been in Coach K's shoes? Explain.

3. What about the story of David and Saul? How would you have handled a situation where someone in authority over you was trying to do you harm?

4. Of the seven people or groups listed that we should respect, with which do you feel like you have generally done a good job? Which ones have you struggled to show respect? Give some examples of each and discuss why some have been more of a challenge than others.

5. Why do you think the concepts of respect, honor and love are so prominently discussed in the Bible?

6. What are some ways you can start showing more respect for others today? How specifically might those acts of respect improve your life and the lives of those around you?

Prayer

Lord, I want to respect You for the awesome Creator you are. I want to show you fear and reverence through the way I live my life. Help me to respect those around me—my family, my friends, my enemies and those in authority—through acts of kindness, forgiveness, humility and love. Let my respect for others be the vehicle that draws them closer to You. Amen.

CHAPTER NINETEEN

FOR THE GLORY OF GOD
Everybody Needs A Higher Purpose

"Whatever you do, do it to glorify God. Use the talents and abilities that He's given you to honor Him." – Kay Yow

When I took over as head boy's basketball coach at Cambridge Rindge and Latin in 1978, the school board and the people throughout the community expected me to lead the team to a state championship. Because of those high expectations, I was driven to prove I was the right person for the job. I wanted to win the championship trophy. I also wanted our team to go undefeated. We did both.

Winning games and championships was only a part of what I wanted to do at Cambridge, and those goals were by no means the most important. I didn't immediately realize that something bigger was going on. In fact, after winning that first state title, there was an empty feeling that I couldn't quite explain.

Certainly there was an immediate, instant excitement and euphoria that came right as the buzzer sounded. I had dreamed about how great it would feel. We huddled up in the locker room and knelt down to thank God. As I left the arena and headed to the bus, it dawned on me that there wouldn't be practice the next day. The season was over, and we wouldn't play again until the next year.

As I matured and grew as a coach, I began to realize that basketball was more about the journey. Winning was important, but it wasn't as important as preparing my players for college and guiding them into a more hopeful future. It was about watching the players grow as athletes and as young men. It was about overcoming a lot of obstacles along the way. It was the relationships that really mattered. That became my focus. That became my motivation.

Even with that acknowledgement, I didn't fully understand the highest purpose behind my role as a coach until a few years later, in an experience that took me half way around the world.

Audience of One

In 2006, I was two years removed from my coaching job at St. John's. More importantly, I was one year into my life as a born-again Christian. While I was uncertain about my professional future, I had great anticipation for what God had in store. I wasn't, however, expecting a phone call from Eric Nelson from Athletes in Action (AIA), a Christian sports organization based in Xenia, Ohio.

AIA had been asked to put a team together for the William Jones Cup, an annual international tournament held in Taipei, Taiwan, that was first played in 1977. Eric wanted to know if I would be interested in coaching the team that consisted of some talented Christian players from various college programs. The thought of coaching again excited me. I had just one request. I wanted my wife Connie to join me on the trip. Eric quickly agreed.

I later learned that my good friend Jim Haney, executive director of the National Association of Basketball Coaches (NABC), had contacted Eric and recommended me for the job. Jim felt it would be a good opportunity for me to get involved in coaching again and spend some quality discipleship time with other Christian coaches.

For seven days in Xenia, I worked with my coaching staff that included Eric, Trent Lehman (also from AIA) and Paul "The Shot Doctor" Maes as we prepared the team for the tournament. At the end of our training session, we packed our bags and took the long flight to Taiwan. By then, we had already bonded into a family unit and were ready to take on the challenge set before us: One Team, One Mission.

The mission was clear. As coaches, we were charged to love our players. The athletes were charged to love each other. Because the team was built on love, the rest of the mission quickly fell into place. We weren't just representing the United States and AIA. We were representing Jesus Christ. We were going to learn about Him. We were going to play for Him. We were going to grow in our relationship with Him. We were going to minister to other teams in His name. It was going to be all about Him.

Although the team played nine games in nine days, we still had time to give coaches clinics and interact with the other coaches and athletes at dinners and during one-on-one time after the games. The team also made time to visit a school for disabled children and a boy's orphanage. We ate with the children. We played with them. We taught them how to play basketball.

The Jones Cup was the biggest thing going on in downtown Taipei, and our hotel was just down the street from the arena. Normally, it would have been a five-minute walk. Instead, it took between 30 to 90 minutes because of all the people that stopped us and wanted autographs from the players and to have their pictures taken with them. The guys probably never felt so much like superstars as they did on that trip. The arena was full every night. It was a big deal.

Before each game, we were given the opportunity to share our testimonies with the crowd. We were ambassadors for our country and our organization, but it almost felt like we were the Apostles going out into the world to share the Gospel.

One night, we met with the coaching staff and the players from Kazakhstan. After sharing the Gospel with them, two players accepted Christ as their Lord and Savior. The team had a tradition that when someone was saved, the others would repeatedly toss the player up into the air and catch him. As you can imagine, this was quite a sight in that small hotel room with low ceilings. I don't know how many tiles got knocked down, but I thought for sure the ceiling was going to come down. It was an incredible night. They huddled, they cried, and they testified to what God had done.

It was also a time of great spiritual growth. Our team chaplain Steve DeBardeladen, and his wife Arlene, led two Bible studies every day. We met once every the morning, before or after practice, and then again at the end of the day. Our Bible studies ended with Rose Maes and Megan Soderberg leading the team in song.

God's Word was a part of everything we did. We probably played really well because we didn't over practice. In fact, we spent more time in Bible study than we did on the court. Yet the games were incredibly competitive, many of which went down to the final seconds. The team played with great energy and passion, not for the crowd or for their individual pride, but for that audience of One.

After we won the championship, the players got their medals and then everybody came together and gave the glory to God. It was one of the most rewarding life experiences I've ever had. It reminded me of what coaching should really be about. Unfortunately, too often we get caught up in all the other stuff.

When James Naismith invented the game of basketball in Springfield, Massachusetts back in 1891, it was meant to enhance education and serve as an evangelistic outreach tool. Basketball was more of a spiritual thing. It was about five people playing together as one for *the* One. That's what we did on our trip to Taiwan. We became one. We had one goal. We had one Head Coach, and it wasn't me. It was never about us. It was all about Him. Everything we did was about fulfilling God's higher purpose and His mission.

All About The Mission

In God's Word, the word "consecration" is used to describe the act of giving everything over to God: mind, body and soul. It's what happens when we see our lives as one continuous act of worship. It's that concept of performing and competing for an audience of One that our team experienced in Taiwan.

In the Old Testament, David spent his early days in the fields watching over his father's flock of sheep. That's also when he wrote songs and sang them to God. We now refer to those songs as Psalms, and they comprise one of the most quoted books of the Bible. Everything David did, from the meadow to the battlefield to the throne room, he did with a heart of consecration. He gave everything to God:

"I will sing of your love and justice; to you, Lord, I will sing praise. I will be careful to lead a blameless life–when will you come to me? I will conduct the affairs of my house with a blameless heart. I will not look with approval on anything that is vile. I hate what faithless people do; I will have no part in it. The perverse of heart shall be far from me; I will have nothing to do with what is evil." (Psalm 101:1-4/NIV)

We see another vivid expression of divine consecration within the story of the early Christian church. In the New Testament book of Acts, we read about how Jesus' disciples became Apostles and led a spiritual revival that would sweep across the globe. They were all about the mission: worshipping God, winning souls, and making disciples. Before Jesus ascended into Heaven, He gave them this empowering message:

"You will receive power when the Holy Spirit comes on you; and you will be my witnesses in Jerusalem, and in all Judea and Samaria, and to the ends of the earth." (Acts 1:8/NIV)

For the next several years, the Apostles dedicated their entire existence to spreading the Gospel to both the Jews and Gentiles. They did so even at their own peril. Giving anything less than everything was not an option, as the Apostle Paul wrote in a letter to the Christians in Rome:

"Therefore, I urge you, brothers and sisters, in view of God's mercy, to offer your bodies as a living sacrifice, holy and pleasing to God–this is your true and proper worship." (Romans 12:1/NIV)

Imagine what our world would be like if we fully consecrated our lives in an act of worship to the audience of One. That is the only way any great acts of faith have ever taken place. It's when the individual or group has sold out completely to God and has wholly committed to doing everything for His glory.

It is that act of surrender that introduces us to His higher purpose and gives us the strength and courage to complete the mission.

Everybody Needs A Higher Purpose

If you accomplish great things, but do so only for your own benefit, you will eventually find yourself empty and unfulfilled. God *wants* you to be fulfilled. That's why He sent His Son Jesus.

"The thief's purpose is to steal and kill and destroy. My purpose is to give them a rich and satisfying life." (John 10:10/NLT)

It might seem contradictory in the natural, but for you to be completely fulfilled, you have to empty yourself, give everything over to God and walk in His higher purpose. Here are three ways you can start living for the glory of God today:

1. Get Low: The first step to stepping into God's higher purpose for your life is to humble yourself and acknowledge that His commandments and His plans are greater than your personal desires.

"Humble yourselves, therefore, under God's mighty hand, that he may lift you up in due time." (1 Peter 5:6/NIV)

2. Lift God High: Surrendering in humility allows us to put God in His proper place and give Him all the glory in the most genuine and authentic way.

"Ascribe to the Lord the glory due His name; worship the Lord in the splendor of His holiness." (Psalm 29:2/NIV)

3. Give God Everything: It's easy to compartmentalize our faith sometimes, but God wants it all. We are called to strive for excellence in our family, at our jobs, in our recreational play and, of course, in our efforts to reach others for Christ. That in and of itself is an act of worship and works towards fulfilling His higher purpose for our lives.

"Whatever you do, do your work heartily, as for the Lord rather than for men." (Colossians 3:23/NAS)

Ultimately, our life's mission and God's higher purpose are synonymous with one another. As we glorify Him in every aspect of our lives, He then opens the doors for us to build His Kingdom through personal evangelism, signs and wonders, and acts of service.

Everybody needs a higher purpose.

Study Questions

1. Think back to a time when you achieved something significant in your life. Did that success fulfill you for an extended period of time or did the sense of accomplishment go away quickly?

2. Have you ever completed a meaningful task or mission with a group of people, perhaps like the AIA team's experience in Taiwan? Was it more or less fulfilling than individual successes you've had in the past? Explain.

3. How often do you think about things like performance, competition, achievement and work as forms of worship to God? What are some other things that might qualify as worship?

4. What does the phrase "audience of One" mean to you? How might looking at worship in that way change the way you approach the many parts of your life?

5. In what ways might pride keep you from fulfilling God's higher purpose? How did David and the Apostles overcome pride, and how might you apply those principles to your life?

6. Read Romans 12:1 and Colossians 3:23. What do you think those scriptures have to do with higher purpose? How do you think your life might change if you were to give everything over to God and do everything for His glory?

Prayer

Lord, I recognize You as the audience of One. No one else matters. All of my thoughts, my actions and my words belong to You. Rid me of my pride so I can lift You up high in my life and begin to fulfill Your higher purpose. I want to reach this world in Your name. I want to help build up Your Kingdom. I want my life to be a reflection of Your glory. Amen.

CHAPTER TWENTY

A UNIVERSAL CALLING
Everybody Needs To Lead

"If your actions inspire others to dream more, learn more, do more and become more, you are a leader." – John Quincy Adams

Some geneticists believe that leaders are born. In other words, they have certain skills and abilities built into their DNA that give them a better chance of becoming a leader. These people are labeled "natural born leaders."

But there are many sociologists who argue the opposite. When listening to their side of the debate, they are often known to say, "Leaders aren't born. They're made."

I think they are *both* right.

There aren't just a select few individuals who are born to lead, but rather all of us have the opportunity to be leaders at some level. How far we take it, however, is dependent on our willingness to submit to authority and learn from the examples of other great leaders.

I wasn't born into a situation that necessarily lent itself to a predestined future as a leader, but thankfully God placed some incredible people in my life who set the examples that I'm still trying to follow today.

Seeing Red

When I was a kid growing up in Cambridge, my older brother Richard used to save up his money and take me to see the Celtics play. I fell in love with the team concept as I watched Bill Russell, Bob Cousy, Sam Jones and that amazing cast of stars work together on the court.

As much as I watched the players, however, I found myself studying head coach Red Auerbach the most. Subconsciously, I was analyzing his demeanor, his game plans and how he put a team together. I didn't realize it at the time, but I was soaking up some incredible knowledge from one of the all-time greats. I also had no idea that eventually I would become close friends with the man simply known as "Red."

In 1973, I joined Tom "Satch" Sanders' staff at Harvard University. Satch was one of the Celtics I watched play for Red in the Garden. For the next four years, we had many conversations about Celtics basketball and how Red coached, conditioned, and inspired his players. That relationship with Satch also opened the door to a friendship with Red.

Over the next several years, I was able to spend some quality time with the Hall of Fame coach on numerous occasions. Whether he viewed it this way or not, Red was an important mentor during the early years of my career.

12 years later, I took my first head coaching college job at Boston University. One night our team hosted a black tie event to raise monies for the basketball program. Red Auerbach was our special guest. As a way of thanking him for his support, I asked my friend Chet Hall, the art teacher at Cambridge Rindge and Latin High School, to create a 4x8 charcoal portrait of Red lighting up his iconic victory cigar. When I presented it to him at the dinner, he was taken aback by the gesture and said he would enjoy having the piece.

The next day, I had my assistant coach Paul Biancardi put the portrait on top of my van and deliver it to Red's office at the Boston Garden.

"What is that?" Red said. "It's too big!"

When Paul called to give me the news, I told him to pack it up and bring it back to my office. That night, I took it home and stored it in my garage. Every day for the next eight months, I would look at Red's portrait when I left for work and when I returned home at the end of the day.

In May of 1990, Connie and I packed the moving vans and left Cambridge for our new job at The George Washington University in Washington D.C. The last thing we loaded into the van was Red's picture. As we arrived at our new home, I was reminded of the fact that Red now lived in D.C. and was one of George Washington's most famous alums. Red started coming to some of my practices.

One day, I had lunch with Red, Jack Kvancz, my athletic director at GW who played for Bob Cousy at Boston College, and my dear friend Bob Chernak, the school's Vice President. Afterward, I asked Red to autograph his portrait for me. He signed his name and added one word: "Win." Red's portrait finally had a home on the wall in our locker room.

Who would have known that at the age of 11, I would be sitting in the Boston Garden idolizing the Celtics and then by the age of 40, I would have a personal relationship with my childhood hero? I often referred to him as my godfather. We would talk about life. We would talk about coaching. At the end of each season, he would sit in my office and we would talk about what it takes to win. Never once did we talk about X's and O's. He always told me it wasn't about that. It was about recruiting good people and learning how to handle them.

"Recruit character, not characters," Red told me in one our meetings.

That may have been one of the best one-liners he ever gave me.

Perhaps the most important thing I learned from Red was how to put a team together. His philosophy was that you had to start with defense. In the end, that's what was going to win championships. The centerpiece for Red was obviously Bill Russell. When we were winning state titles at Cambridge, my centerpiece was Patrick Ewing. I tried to coach Patrick the same way Red coached Bill, as a true center who did whatever it took to help his team to win.

After the center, the most important position was the point guard. Red had Bob Cousy and K.C. Jones. At Cambridge, I had Kevin Moore, Charlie Neal and Rumeal Robinson.

Then there was the role of the sixth man, a concept Red introduced to the NBA. Whenever possible, I tried to pattern my team around the idea that you needed a great player who was willing to provide a spark off the bench. Everybody wants to start. Everybody wants to be the star. But Red had a way of selling the concept to future Hall of Fame players like Frank Ramsey, Sam Jones, and John Havlicek.

Red's sixth man concept worked in my first season at Cambridge when one of my top five players, David Dottin, helped us bring home our first state championship. That same philosophy especially made a difference the year I convinced Rumeal Robinson to come off the bench. Rumeal was one of the top 10 players in the country. He went on to become an All-American at Cambridge and in college at Michigan. Rumeal famously made the game-winning free throws against Seton Hall that secured the Wolverines' 1989 NCAA Championship.

Apart from Red's elite team management skills, he was a beloved coach, thanks to a deep commitment and connection to his players. He listened to them. He knew what made them tick. He worked hard to earn their trust and respect.

I saw this firsthand in his relationship with Satch Sanders. Red would make regular visits to the Harvard campus and climb five sets of stairs to attend our practices on the fifth floor of our indoor athletic building. He would sit on a wooden chair at half court for the entire practice just to support one of his former players.

Red had a great deal of confidence and wasn't afraid to show it. To most, he came off as arrogant, but deep down, he was a kind and gentle man. The first time I met Red was when we were standing next to each other in the men's room at the Basketball Hall of Fame.

"Hey kid," he said. "That player of yours, that Ewing kid, he's going to be in the NBA someday."

And then he said something else that I'll never forget.

"I may not always be right, but I've never been wrong."

A Servant Leader

From 1986 to 1997, I served as a board member for the National Association of Basketball Coaches (NABC). In my last year on the board, I served as president. During those last five years, I had the opportunity to work with and learn from another great leader, Jim Haney, our executive director.

Jim coached at Oregon from 1978 to 1983 and spent some time as an assistant coach at Kansas. He was also the commissioner of the Missouri Valley Conference for three years, but it was a move to the NABC where Jim's leadership skills truly began to shine.

First and foremost, I learned from Jim that great leaders are smart and have a lot of common sense. The most successful leaders, though, are compassionate and live to serve others. I've seen him hire former coaches like Ernie Kent and Reggie Minton to reward them for their dedication and loyalty to the game. Thanks to Jim and a job well done, Ernie returned to coaching at Washington State. Reggie became Jim's right hand man as the deputy director of the NABC.

Jim showed that same compassion for me after I was fired at St. John's. I wasn't sure what was next for me, but Jim took the time to talk to me about my future. He, like Red, was a great listener. After he listened to me and felt my pain, Jim gave me some sound advice and some scriptures to chew on. When Jim spoke, I could feel his deep love and concern. When he referred to me as his brother, he meant it.

Jim often spoke about how much God loves me and how I had to believe God's plan was better than mine. Jim made it possible for me to stay actively involved in college basketball when he asked me to serve on the NABC Foundation Board. A year later, he worked behind the scenes and convinced Eric Nelson to offer me the opportunity to coach the Athletes in Action team that represented the United States in the Jones Cup in Taiwan. It was a life-changing experience.

From Jim's example, I also learned that great leaders are mentors. They are intentional in building meaningful relationships with those within their circle of influence. I've seen Jim mentor young and old coaches alike. Any time I've needed to deal with a personal or professional issue, he has always been there for me. If he doesn't pick up the phone when I call, I know I will get a return call soon.

In order to be a great leader, you also have to be bold. You have to be willing to stand up for what you believe. That's another thing that I admire about Jim; in his attempt to build and develop the NABC, he has always put God first. When he speaks, it's not about him. It's about what's best for the game, the coaches, and the players. He speaks the truth and goes out of his way to give credit where credit is due, and that always includes God.

On many occasions, I've heard him mention the name of Jesus, which most people today are afraid to do because it's not politically correct. Jim has put chills up and down my spine when sharing the Gospel at our annual Final Four gatherings. He is an incredibly emotional, spiritual, passionate, and humble leader.

Most of the time, you don't even know that Jim is the one who is making things happen. He is truly a servant leader who would rather stand in the back of the room and allow others to get the credit. That's another reason people like Ernie Kent and Reggie Minton love to work for Jim.

Jim's boldness has bled into his vision for the NABC. For years, going to the Final Four was all about the games, the meetings and the clinics. But when Jim took the reins, he made it possible for Athletes in Action and Fellowship of Christian Athletes to have a vibrant place where families, married couples and coaches could fellowship with one another. For many others and me, those gatherings have become the best events at the Final Four.

How is Jim Haney able to lead with such compassion, conviction and vision? It's simple. He knows who *his* leader is.

To be a great leader, you have to be a great follower. You have to pick great people to follow. I've been able to stand behind Jim and watch how he works with other people. Yet at the same time, it's very obvious who is directing Jim and who his head coach is.

Jim Haney follows Jesus Christ.

Everybody Needs To Lead

We are all followers. Yet we are all leaders. This is one of life's great paradoxes. There's always someone in authority over us: parents, teachers, coaches, government officials, administrators, pastors, God, etc., but there is also always someone we have the ability to influence (spouses, children, friends, co-workers, teammates, students, etc.)

Whether we are the leader for one person or many people, it's important to understand the value of our individual leadership opportunities. While it would take an entire book to discuss all of the characteristics a great leader should display, here are five key principles I learned from Red and Jim that can help all of us more effectively embrace our inner leader:

1. Put Others First: This is counter to what current culture says about leadership. It's not uncommon these days for leaders to experience a sense of entitlement, but a great leader understands that putting other's needs first will develop unbreakable bonds, greater efficiency within the larger group, and a better chance at achieving a common goal. Being a servant leader is also far more rewarding than allowing selfishness, ego and greed to take charge.

"Do nothing out of selfish ambition or vain conceit. Rather, in humility value others above yourselves, not looking to your own interests but each of you to the interests of the others." (Philippians 2:3-4/NIV)

2. Have a Plan: It's impossible to lead someone if you don't know where you're going. Before setting out on a journey, make sure to have a plan that is easily explained and easily followed. Make it a bold plan, but more importantly make sure it is a *divinely inspired* plan.

"Many are the plans in a person's heart, but it is the Lord's purpose that prevails." (Proverbs 19:21/NIV)

3. Listen Up: The best leaders are good listeners. They listen to and pay close attention to what those under their leadership have to say. They also seek out the advice of wise, seasoned leaders and peers who can help keep them accountable and look out for their blind spots.

"Tune your ears to wisdom, and concentrate on understanding." (Proverbs 2:2/NLT)

4. Stay True To Your Convictions: Not many things are more pathetic than a wishy-washy leader. Know what you believe and stick to your guns. Otherwise, the foundation below your feet will be on shaky ground at best. It's hard to stand on principles that are constantly shifting and changing. Great leaders don't have to work too hard to defend their actions. They know *what* they are doing and *why* they are doing it.

"Be on your guard; stand firm in the faith; be courageous; be strong." (1 Corinthians 16:13/NIV)

5. Follow the Leader: Jesus was the greatest leader ever. He was the ultimate model of service and compassion. He was also a willing mentor and bold visionary who never strayed from His message of hope, faith and love. Being a great leader can be as simple as following His perfect example.

"To this you were called, because Christ suffered for you, leaving you an example, that you should follow in his steps." (1 Peter 2:21/NIV)

We are all natural born leaders, but we are also compelled to embrace that universal calling and diligently seek out ways to develop our God-given leadership abilities and step boldly into the opportunities God has set before us.

Everybody needs to lead.

Study Questions

1. Do you consider yourself a leader? Explain.

2. If you answered yes to the previous question, do you believe you were born with leadership abilities, that you learned them through life experiences, or it was a combination of both?

3. Who are some leaders who have taught you about leadership? What are some things about leadership you learned from them?

4. In what areas of your life would you consider yourself a leader? Are there some areas where you feel like you need to step up and do a better job? Explain.

5. What do you believe are the most important keys to being a great leader? Which of these characteristics do you have? Which ones need to be developed more in your life?

6. What are some of Jesus' characteristics that have inspired you most as a leader? What are some things you can start to do today that will help you better follow His example?

Prayer

Lord, thank you for calling me to be a leader. Help me to better see where you want me to step up and accept my role as a leader. Put people in my life that will help me be a better leader. I want to follow Jesus closely so that I might lead like Him. Amen.

CHAPTER TWENTY-ONE

ETERNAL IMPACT
Everybody Needs To Leave A Legacy

"It is not the honor that you take with you, but the heritage you leave behind." – Branch Rickey

David Nicholas may not be the most famous person with whom I've crossed paths, but he has unquestionably been one of the most important and influential.

Pastor Nicholas didn't believe anything happened by chance. It was never about luck. It was always about being blessed. If I said I was lucky or that we were lucky as a team, he would give me a mini-sermon on God's blessings.

After a while, I learned not to use that word, but not in time to avoid a comical situation that took place at a restaurant where my wife Connie and I were having dinner with Pastor Nicholas and his wife Nori. We were standing outside waiting for our table when I made the mistake of telling David how our team had been lucky to win a recent game. This resulted in a 10-minute lecture. I really got an earful.

At some point, I started a conversation with David's wife while Connie began talking with David. Wouldn't you know, Connie made the same mistake and talked about being lucky! True to form, David gave her the same lecture I had received just a few minutes earlier.

When we finally got to our table, our waitress came over to take our orders. She was a very pleasant young lady and had a great sense of humor. As I often do at other restaurants, I asked the waitress her name. We all laughed hysterically when she gave her response:

"My name is Lucky."

Pastor Nicholas laughed, shook his head, and didn't say a word.

Our waitress was the only one that evening who didn't get a lecture about luck.

God Thinks Big

I didn't realize it at the time, but my predestined relationship with David Nicholas was set into motion on December 19, 2003. That was the day St. John's University relieved me of my duties as the men's basketball coach. Connie and I decided it would be in our best interest to move as far away from New York City as possible and start fresh in a completely different environment.

Because Connie had gone through so much turmoil in those last few months at St. John's, I felt she deserved the opportunity to choose where we would live. She wanted to move to a warmer climate, somewhere near the kids. Through a process of elimination, she chose Florida.

We had no idea how life-changing the decision would ultimately be. As was customary when we moved to a new city, the first order of business was to find a church home. After two failed attempts to find an A.M.E. Church, my wife suggested we visit Spanish River Church, which was less than five minutes from our home.

The details of how I met Pastor Nicholas and how he led me into a personal relationship with Christ can be found in the Afterword (Meet My Head Coach, p. 237). But for this chapter, I want to focus on an important biblical principle he consistently taught and modeled and how it has changed the way I view my place within the Body of Christ.

There were a couple of things you knew you could expect from David. First and foremost, you were always going to hear the Gospel, or as he referred to it, "the bad news and the good news." Secondly, you were always going to get recruited to help him plant churches.

It wasn't enough for David to have a successful, vibrant church. David knew his church was just a seed. He wanted to spread the

Word and grow the faith through church plants. Almost 20 percent of what Spanish River Church takes in through tithes and offerings goes to the Church Planting Network that David founded. In 2014 alone, almost two million dollars went toward that effort. All told, Pastor Nicholas' vision has been responsible for at least 425 churches in 12 countries including Tim Keller's vibrant Redeemer Presbyterian Church in Manhattan.

Not surprisingly, David made sure his two biggest points of emphasis were working together in concert. The pastors of his church plants were, and are still, required to preach the Gospel every week. For many years, David ran spiritual boot camps to teach ministry staffs how to incorporate the Gospel into every sermon and every service. His wife Nori is now finishing the job that he started.

"God thinks big!" he always told me.

Looking at the results of David's efforts, it's obvious that statement was true.

In 2011, I was the head basketball coach at Florida Atlantic University. On January 22, ESPN2 broadcast our only televised game that season. I invited Pastor Nicholas to be my special guest and sit on the bench during the game. There he was, in his favorite black leather suit jacket, as our team defeated the University of Arkansas at Little Rock, 88-71.

On the way back to the locker room at halftime, David stopped me and said, "Coach, I'm getting phone calls and text messages like you wouldn't believe! People are seeing me on television! I'm a big shot!"

In that moment, David's zest for life and innocent exuberance truly shined through.

Three days later, on January 25, 2011, David died of cardiac arrest, just a few hours after teaching a seminar for 25 pastors. My dear friend was 79 years old when he passed away. When we got to the hospital, he was still in the room. He had a calm, peaceful look on his face.

Although it seemed like David still had so much left to do, it was reassuring to think about all the seeds he had planted across the community, across the nation, across the globe and, just as importantly, within the Spanish River Church congregation.

At the memorial service, the auditorium was completely full and the service was broadcast in the chapel for those who couldn't find a seat. Sr. Pastor Tom Kiedis preached an inspirational and challenging message. You could see tears rolling down people's cheeks, mine included. There was no way to know how many had come to Christ through David's ministry, but we got a very small sampling when Pastor Kiedis asked any such person in the congregation to stand up.

As I rose to my feet and looked around, it seemed like half the church was standing and crying with me.

Two years before David's death, he began the transition process and began preparing and mentoring his replacement, Tommy Kiedis, who now serves as senior pastor. David knew what a lasting legacy was supposed to look like. Legacies should outlive us. Legacies should continue to grow and get bigger, even after the original builder has died.

Pastor Nicholas inspired me in many ways. Before I'm gone, I want to plant at least one church in his honor. I'm confident David would feel blessed, not lucky, if he were able to see that dream of mine come true.

Spiritual Ancestors

During Jesus' time on Earth, He didn't come to build the Christian church. He came to lay its foundation and plant the seeds that would help it grow. Jesus didn't have to become the greatest church planter who ever lived. That's because He mentored and discipled the people who would become the Church's spiritual ancestors. Jesus left that incredible legacy to the Apostles.

We can learn a great deal about legacy and how we can live one of our own by looking at what the Apostles did in the wake of Jesus' death, resurrection and ascension back to Heaven.

They had a vision. The Apostles didn't always agree on everything. They, in fact, had some theological differences. But nothing could dissuade them from the calling Jesus gave them:

"Therefore go and make disciples of all nations, baptizing them in the name of the Father and of the Son and of the Holy Spirit, and teaching them to obey everything I have commanded you. And surely I am with you always, to the very end of the age." (Matthew 28:19-20/NIV)

They didn't worry about who got the credit. A legacy built on pride won't last. It will ultimately crumble and fall apart. Humility, on the other hand, provides a solid foundation that cannot be easily shaken. The Apostle Paul explained this principle in one of his letters to the church in Corinth where jealousy and quarreling were becoming a problem amongst the believers. He used his working relationship with another Christian leader to make his point:

"I planted the seed, Apollos watered it, but God has been making it grow." (1 Corinthians 3:6/NIV)

They were fully committed. The Apostles knew that their calling would likely put them in harm's way. They understood there would be great opposition to the Gospel message, but because they had a vision and were fully invested in that vision, they were willing to go the distance, even if that meant laying down their mortal bodies. As Paul solemnly conveyed in his farewell to the Ephesian elders:

"I consider my life worth nothing to me; my only aim is to finish the race and complete the task the Lord Jesus has given me–the task of testifying to the good news of God's grace." (Acts 20:24/NIV)

If you apply those principles to your life's work, your legacy will not only survive, it will flourish, expand and have eternal value.

Everybody Needs To Leave A Legacy

God has called each of us to have a legacy and to leave the world in a better place than what we found it. For the Apostles, that meant giving their lives to spread the Gospel and build up the Body of Christ. For David Nicholas, that meant planting churches all over the world. My legacy is still a work in progress. It involves using basketball and my story as a tool to impact people's lives for the Kingdom. It also has everything to do with my responsibilities as a husband, father and grandfather.

You might have a different legacy in the works. Or maybe you don't have much of a legacy to speak of at this point in your life. That's okay. It's never too late to start planting seeds and building a legacy that will last long after you are gone. Here are three simple ways to get your legacy going and to keep it growing:

1. Think big, start small: Like my friend Pastor Nicholas, you should think big because God thinks big. But you don't have to start big. In fact, more often, you will need to start small and build from there. You might impact millions of lives one day, but in the meantime, look around you and find one individual or a small group of people you can serve, encourage and mentor. You shouldn't have to look too far. Familiar settings such as your family, your job and your church can provide rich opportunities. As you prove faithful, God will surely bless you with greater influence and a solid foundation upon which you can build your legacy.

"Whoever can be trusted with very little can also be trusted with much." (Luke 16:10a/NIV)

2. Don't grow weary: Legacy building requires patience. It takes time. Throughout the daily grind, it can become easy to slack off on doing those things that matter most. This is true for us as parents. This is true for us as employers and employees. This is also true for us as Christians and community servants, but no legacy worth its salt has ever come easy. Fight through the hard times and see what God can do with your effort.

"For the one who sows to his own flesh will from the flesh reap corruption, but the one who sows to the Spirit will from the Spirit reap eternal life. Let us not lose heart in doing good, for in due time we will reap if we do not grow weary." (Galatians 6:8-9/NIV)

3. See the eternal value: Building a legacy isn't about having a good name or leaving behind monuments by which people will remember you. It's about making an impact on others in both the here and now and in the afterlife. What we do today can literally change people's lives forever.

"Don't store up treasures here on earth, where moths eat them and rust destroys them, and where thieves break in and steal. Store your treasures in heaven, where moths and rust cannot destroy, and thieves do not break in and steal." (Matthew 6:19-20/NLT)

Your legacy might be your children. It might be your ministry. Perhaps your legacy is your business. Or maybe it's a cause for which you have diligently fought. What's most important to recognize is the fact that God has called you to fulfill that legacy and it's up to you to nurture and diligently work to preserve it for His glory.

Everybody needs to leave a legacy.

Study Questions

1. What comes to mind when you think of the word "legacy?"

2. How often do you think about what kind of legacy you are leaving behind? If you could pre-determine your legacy today, what do you hope it would look like?

3. Who are some historical figures you would say left behind lasting legacies and why? Who are some people close to you that left behind lasting legacies and how has that impacted your life?

4. In discussing the Apostles, we mentioned three reasons why they left behind such long-lasting legacies. Which of those reasons (vision, humility and commitment) have helped you build a firm foundation? Which have you struggled to incorporate in your legacy building process?

5. What do phrases like "eternal value" and "eternal impact" mean to you? How should those concepts shape your idea of a lasting legacy?

6. What are some things you have already done to build a legacy for your family, your church, your community, etc.? What are some things you haven't done yet or could try to do better?

Prayer

Lord, thank You for the blessing of legacy. Thank You for the people whose legacy has made a difference in my life. Help me to see each day as an opportunity to leave a legacy behind for my family, my friends, my co-workers, my church family, my community and my world. I want to have an eternal impact on everyone that crosses my path. Amen.

CHAPTER TWENTY-TWO

WHEN AMERICA IS BEAUTIFUL
Everybody Needs Community

"Alone we can do so little; together we can do so much." – Helen Keller

In 2013, The Weinstein Company released *The Butler*, a historical drama loosely based on the life of Eugene Allen, who worked in the White House as a waiter and butler for 34 years. In the film, Allen's character was renamed Cecil Gaines and portrayed by Forest Whitaker. *The Butler* also touted an all-star cast that included Oprah Winfrey, John Cusack, Cuba Gooding Jr., and Robin Williams.

Connie and I saw the movie twice. While I enjoyed the film the first time, the historical content didn't hit home until my second viewing. I became much more emotional as the events that took place between 1952 and 1986 unfolded. Allen first worked in the White House during the Eisenhower administration and continued until his retirement during Ronald Regan's presidency. It was as if I were watching my own life on the big screen. So much of what happened during that time period was a reflection of the major events that shaped who I am today.

I was born toward the end of World War II. I have lived through the Korean War, the Vietnam War, the Gulf War, the 9-11 attacks, and the subsequent conflicts in Afghanistan and Iraq. These events have become an inseparable part of my life experience.

One thing that always stood out, especially during those earlier wars, America was at its best when its people felt as if they were under attack. The concept of community, or working together for a common goal, was fully embraced and exercised. The same has been true in those tragic moments when some of our leaders have been assassinated.

On November 22, 1963, President John F. Kennedy was shot and killed in Dallas, Texas, while traveling in a presidential motorcade with his wife Jacqueline and Texas Governor John Connally and his wife Nellie. I was a freshman at Northeastern University on that infamous day. In the weeks that followed, Americans united: blacks and whites, rich people and poor people. Many tears were shed as all citizens committed to the wellbeing of our country.

A few years later, Connie and I marched in Boston during a civil rights march with Martin Luther King. I can remember walking down Columbus Avenue, holding my future wife's hand on one side and holding a white person's hand on the other side. MLK united people of all colors and socio-economic statuses. Through his leadership, many Americans put race and color aside and came together for the good of the country. He wanted what God wanted, for all people to love one another.

Martin Luther King's "I Have A Dream" speech still resonates in the hearts and minds of all people. Sadly, one of the lasting memories in my mind took place on April 4, 1968. My wife and I were attending a banquet with many of my former college teammates when we were informed that MLK had been shot and killed in Memphis, Tennessee, at the Lorraine Motel.

Two months and one day later, on June 5, 1968, my brother Stephen and I watched television news coverage of the assassination of Robert F. Kennedy at the Ambassador Hotel in Los Angeles after winning the California Democratic Party's Presidential primary. Kennedy was perceived by many to be the only person in either party who was capable of uniting the country. He, like his brother John, was beloved by the black community because of his devotion to the civil rights cause. RFK had hoped to continue what his brother had started. His death served as another unifying event during one of our country's most tumultuous times.

The City of Squares

I was born April 11, 1945 in Cambridge, Massachusetts.

Cambridge is known for being home to Harvard University and Massachusetts Institute of Technology (MIT), two prestigious institutions of higher learning. The city of Cambridge was first settled in 1630 and is one of the oldest cities in the United States. If you ever visit my hometown, you'll probably notice its unique design. Cambridge, in fact, is often referred to as "The City of Squares" because of how the major street intersections are laid out. These squares (Harvard Square, Kendall Square, Central Square, etc.) serve as neighborhood centers.

The city of Boston is just across the Charles River to the south. Boston was very segregated and divided back then. It had separate city halls for its different constituencies, but Cambridge was different. Cambridge represented what America was supposed to be about. You could go into just about any neighborhood and feel safe. Blacks and whites lived together throughout most of the communities. Even though I lived in a community that was predominantly black, I played ball with and went to school with white kids. We were totally integrated. It wasn't forced integration but rather something that happened naturally.

As I got older, I started to see that things were much more separate than what I had originally believed. It wasn't until I ventured outside of Cambridge that I started to hear the n-word and other racial epithets. I also started to learn that race is often a tool used within political parties as a way to gain influence and power. Today, there are still too many cities and states divided along racial and socio-economic lines. It's a far cry from the first national election I can remember, when Dwight D. Eisenhower was running for President. Back then there were no blue state or red states. It was simply the United States.

America wasn't perfect, but it was beautiful. I didn't have to look far for some powerful examples of that beauty.

When I was 11 years old, my brother Richard took me to my first Celtics game. We made regular visits to the Boston Garden throughout my adolescent and teenage years. What I observed was a white Jewish coach who didn't care about color. Red Auerbach wanted the best players and the best people. He built his teams around talent and character. Red also didn't care too much about what others thought about him and his decisions.

On December 26, 1964, in the midst of a racially charged city and era, Red Auerbach became the first coach to start five black players in an NBA game. I was 19 years old and remember hearing the historic moment unfold on the radio. The Celtics were on the road playing the St. Louis Hawks. Willie Naulls replaced regular starter Tommy Heinsohn, who was injured, and joined Bill Russell, Satch Sanders, K.C. Jones and Sam Jones as Boston came away with the victory, 97-84.

Two days later, I was in the Boston Garden when that same starting lineup made its debut in front of the hometown crowd. In a high-scoring affair, the Celtics defeated the Los Angeles Lakers, 133-112. Those two teams would meet again in the 1965 NBA Finals where Boston's 4-1 series win earned the organization its seventh consecutive championship.

When Red became Boston's general manager, he made history again when he hired the NBA's first African-American head coach. Bill Russell and the Celtics continued to win championships and show sports fans across the country what was possible when people were judged on their ability and not the color of their skin.

The power of community hit even closer to home during "The Blizzard of '78," a catastrophic nor'easter that dumped 27 inches of snow on the Boston Metropolitan area. The blizzard lasted from February 5 until February 7, but the effects were felt nearly two weeks after the storm had passed. Many people were stranded in their cars on the highway. Thousands of Boston University hockey fans were forced to hole up inside the Boston Garden. The storm caused over $520 million in damage and tragically took approximately 100 lives throughout the Northeastern United States.

Thankfully, we were at home in North Cambridge when the blizzard hit. Mike Jr., was nine years old at the time; Dana was eight. The governor declared a state of emergency and banned all forms of transportation. All of a sudden, the people in our neighborhood were drawn together. We looked out for each other and made sure everyone had what they needed to weather the storm.

In a genuine act of community, everyone gathered whatever food they had in their houses and brought it next door to Bill Kelly's house. Bill fired up his grill and hosted cookouts that not only provided much needed sustenance but a reprieve from the calamitous happenings in our city.

A Common Enemy

Like the many wars and natural disasters this nation has endured, community happens much easier when we are facing a common enemy or dealing with large-scale tragedies and challenging circumstances. Perhaps there has been no better example of this truth than on September 11, 2001 when the United States was faced with the horrors of terrorism on its own soil.

Like so many Americans, I'll never forget where I was on that fateful day. I was in the St. John's locker room with my managers, preparing a morning snack for our team. We were making peanut butter and jelly sandwiches on bagels, getting out some cereal and fruit, and pouring orange juice, just like any other morning. Then, one of the managers came to me and asked if I'd seen what was going on. Until that moment, I had no idea that a plane had flown into one of the World Trade Center towers. A few minutes later, we were gathered around the television and saw the second plane fly into the other tower.

Word spread quickly. School was cancelled. The players started coming into my office to talk about what was happening. Many of them were crying; all of them were very upset. To make matters worse, parents were frantically calling to check on their kids. Since Madison Square Garden was our basketball home, many people were concerned about our safety. The main campus, however, is located thirty minutes outside of Manhattan in Queens. We were safely distanced from the mayhem, but it was a troubling situation nonetheless.

A few days later, my wife and I ventured into the city to see the devastation firsthand. A New York policeman recognized me and allowed us to see the rubble at Ground Zero. We saw the huge holes in the ground. The area was full of ash, smoke and bodies that had not yet been extracted; the awful smell of burnt flesh filled the air. It was an unbelievable sight.

Ironically, our wedding anniversary is September 9th. A year earlier on that date, Connie and I celebrated at Windows of the World, which was at the top of the North Tower (also referred to as Building One) on the 107th floor. I remember looking out across Manhattan. It was an incredible sight. I also remember asking my wife an ominous and, at the time, seemingly rhetorical question.

"Can you imagine being up here if a fire broke out?"

A year and two days later, we watched as the building came tumbling down; a day that forever changed America.

In the days and weeks following the attacks, our country came together like never before. We focused our attention on one enemy and the healing and rebuilding of our nation. In doing so, we rallied behind our government officials. We rallied behind our first responders. We rallied behind our military. We rallied behind our spiritual leaders. We rallied together to serve each other and more importantly to pray for those whom the tragedy had directly impacted.

Our nation is still recovering from the events of 9-11. The United States of America has never been the same, but one good thing did come out of the tragedy. Once again, the American people united, and it was truly one for all and all for one. Yes, the government was vitally important in the country's recovery, but at the end of the day, it was really about people, not programs. It was about neighbors helping neighbors. It was about churches reaching out into the communities. It was about individual people being there for those around them.

People prayed for one another. People individually and collectively made an effort to garner the spirit that makes America great.

The blessing of those terrorist attacks on 9-11 was that we were reminded of how fragile life is and how much we need each other. It showed us what community should really look like.

A Common Cause

In the Book of Acts, we read about the early Christians and how they built the Church from the ground up. While we often focus on their evangelistic work, we sometimes forget that they gave us a beautiful example of divinely inspired community.

So what exactly did they do that helped them lay the foundation and expand the Body of Christ in the face of great adversity and dire persecution? Here are 10 specific actions that were highly beneficial to creating community within the early Church:

They were committed to a common cause: The early Christians were all in. They knew their lives were on the line, but because they had a common cause, they were able to lock arms and work together for the greater good, which was the call that Jesus gave just before ascending into Heaven:

"Therefore go and make disciples of all nations, baptizing them in the name of the Father and of the Son and of the Holy Spirit, and teaching them to obey everything I have commanded you. And surely I am with you always, to the very end of the age." (Matthew 28:19-20/NIV)

They met each other's needs: The early Christians believed Jesus was returning in their lifetime. Already committed to each other as a tight-knit community, this caused them to take even more extreme measures to ensure that everyone's needs were adequately met.

"And all the believers met together in one place and shared everything they had. They sold their property and possessions and shared the money with those in need." (Acts 2:44/NIV)

They reached out to those around them: The early Christians remembered what Jesus had taught about serving others and put those lessons into practice. They administered food and drink to the less fortunate, visited prisoners and took care of widows and orphans.

"Don't forget to show hospitality to strangers, for some who have done this have entertained angels without realizing it! Remember those in prison, as if you were there yourself. Remember also those being mistreated, as if you felt their pain in your own bodies...And don't forget to do good and to share with those in need. These are the sacrifices that please God." (Hebrews 13:2-3, 16/NLT)

They had authentic, loving relationships: Jesus told His disciples that the world would know they were His followers because of the love they showed one another (John 13:35). The early Christians took this to heart and practiced real, authentic love within their communities.

"Don't just pretend to love others. Really love them. Hate what is wrong. Hold tightly to what is good. Love each other with genuine affection, and take delight in honoring each other." (Romans 12:9-10/NIV)

They prayed for one another: As an offshoot of those authentic, loving relationships, the early Christians were encouraged to take each other's needs to God in prayer. The Apostle Paul demonstrated this often in his letters to the early Christians, including this message to the believers in Philippi:

"I thank my God every time I remember you. In all my prayers for all of you, I always pray with joy because of your partnership in the gospel from the first day until now, being confident of this, that he who began a good work in you will carry it on to completion until the day of Christ Jesus." (Philippians 1:3-6/NIV)

They stayed connected: The early Christians couldn't afford to become isolated. There was too much at stake. They regularly met for worship, prayer, fellowship, discipleship, and service (Acts 2:42). This was vital for the Church's growth and for the believers' survival.

"Let us think of ways to motivate one another to acts of love and good works. And let us not neglect our meeting together, as some people do, but encourage one another, especially now that the day of his return is drawing near." (Hebrews 10:24-25/NIV)

They embraced their roles: No one was terribly concerned about who was in charge and who was assigned the many responsibilities within the various communities. The early Church understood that every part was important, as the Apostle Paul so deftly taught in his letter to the Christians in Rome.

"Just as our bodies have many parts and each part has a special function, so it is with Christ's body. We are many parts of one body, and we all belong to each other.

In his grace, God has given us different gifts for doing certain things well. So if God has given you the ability to prophesy, speak out with as much faith as God has given you. If your gift is serving others, serve them well. If you are a teacher, teach well. If your gift is to encourage others, be encouraging. If it is giving, give generously. If God has given you leadership ability, take the responsibility seriously. And if you have a gift for showing kindness to others, do it gladly." (Romans 12:4-8/NIV)

They kept the peace: It would have been easy for the early Christians to want to rise up and fight against those who were attacking them for their faith. They were being persecuted on a daily basis. As time went on, those outside attacks turned increasingly violent and resulted in countless martyrs. Even still, they resisted the temptation to strike back and instead followed the Apostle Paul's divinely influenced call for peace.

"Do not repay anyone evil for evil. Be careful to do what is right in the eyes of everyone. If it is possible, as far as it depends on you, live at peace with everyone. Do not take revenge, my dear friends, but leave room for God's wrath, for it is written: 'It is mine to avenge; I will repay,' says the Lord." (Romans 12:17-19/NIV)

They resisted negative influences: The early Christians weren't concerned about what people outside of their community thought about them. They didn't allow verbal attacks, accusations or secular worldviews to infiltrate their circle. Instead, they did their best to adhere to the Apostle Paul's teaching regarding godly living.

"Don't copy the behavior and customs of this world, but let God transform you into a new person by changing the way you think. Then you will learn to know God's will for you, which is good and pleasing and perfect." (Romans 12:2/NLT)

They stood on common ground: The early Christians agreed on the most important things. They agreed Jesus was God's Son and that He died on the Cross and rose again on the third day. They also agreed there was only one true God and that salvation was only available through His grace. That was their common ground.

Although they didn't agree on some lesser important theological issues (Paul and Peter, for instance, had a minor dispute referenced in Galatians 2:11-14) that didn't stop them from working together for the singular cause of spreading the Good News throughout the world. Even before His death and resurrection, Jesus prayed that this would come to pass.

"My prayer is not for them alone. I pray also for those who will believe in me through their message, that all of them may be one, Father, just as you are in me and I am in you. May they also be in us so that the world may believe that you have sent me. I have given them the glory that you gave me, that they may be one as we are one—I in them and you in me—so that they may be brought to complete unity. Then the world will know that you sent me and have loved them even as you have loved me." (John 17:20-23/NIV)

The early Church was not perfect. It was made up of flawed humans who assuredly made plenty of mistakes along the way. But their example of community is something we can and should learn from today.

Everybody Needs Community

America is at its best when people work together for a common goal. Community can take place in extended families, neighborhoods, towns, cities, states, and, as was shown during the aftermath of 9-11, throughout the nation. Community should especially be practiced and exhibited within the local church and throughout the global Body of Christ.

Here are four ways you can start building community wherever you might be:

1. Get plugged in: Get out there and find out what is going on around you. It's impossible to create community if you don't make yourself available to spend time with your neighbors, your city leaders and your fellow churchgoers. If you don't commune with others, you will never be able to help build and grow community.

"One who has isolated himself seeks his own selfish desires; he rejects all sound judgment." (Proverbs 18:1/NET)

2. Diversify your portfolio: Don't get stuck hanging out in the same circles. Perhaps you've been limited in the kinds of people with which you associate. Be intentional about it and expand your horizons to include individuals and groups that are from different racial and socio-economic backgrounds. After all, we are all one in God's eyes.

"There is no longer Jew or Gentile, slave or free, male and female. For you are all one in Christ Jesus." (Galatians 3:28/NLT)

3. Find common ground: In Cambridge, we came together to support our schools, our athletic teams and our arts programs. We also came together to help each other deal with adversity. In our nation, we came together to fight a common enemy and pick up the pieces after natural disasters and tragedies. In the early Church, the Jews worked together with Gentiles to spread the Gospel message and build up the body of Christ. If God's love is your guide, you can do the same thing wherever you call home.

"Therefore, as God's chosen people, holy and dearly loved, clothe yourselves with compassion, kindness, humility, gentleness and patience. Bear with each other and forgive one another if any of you has a grievance against someone. Forgive as the Lord forgave you. And over all these virtues put on love, which binds them all together in perfect unity." (Colossians 3:12-14/NIV)

4. Don't wait for tragedy: It shouldn't take a natural disaster, a terrorist attack or a war to bring people together. Don't wait for catastrophic events to take place before building relationships and creating community within your life.

"Don't be fools; be wise: make the most of every opportunity you have for doing good." (Ephesians 5:15/TLB)

America is still beautiful, and so is the Body of Christ. But think about how much more beautiful both could become if they were to return to the original models of community upon which they were built.

Everybody needs community.

Study Questions

1. What does the word "community" mean to you? Describe a time when you experienced community in your personal life.

2. Why do you think community often takes place during times of tragedy and great adversity?

3. What do you think are some obstacles to community in today's modern age? What are some ways we might be able to overcome some of those obstacles as a society?

4. Of the 10 examples of community shown by the Early Church, which ones do you think we tend to struggle with today? Why do you think that's the case?

5. Go back and look at the four keys to creating community in your own life. Which of those do you feel like you've been able to do relatively well? Which of those do you need to improve upon?

6. What are some things you can start doing today that will help you better create community in your neighborhood, your church, and your hometown?

Prayer

Lord, I want to do my part to bring a stronger sense of community back to my circle of influence. Help me find common ground with those around me. Help me step outside of my comfort zone and reach out to those who need help, even those who are different than me. Help me to not wait for tragedy but to begin looking for ways to create community even when things seem to be going well. I want others to know that I am Your disciple because of my love for them. Amen.

CHAPTER TWENTY-THREE

MOVING FORWARD
Everybody Needs Grace

"The meaning of life. The wasted years of life. The poor choices of life. God answers the mess of life with one word: 'grace.'" – Max Lucado

Grace is one of those words that can mean different things to different people depending on the given circumstances. Some might refer to grace as effortless beauty and charm. Others might think of grace as generosity and goodwill. Still others might define the word as mercy or reprieve.

Those are all great definitions, but my favorite one is simply "God's unmerited favor towards man."

Another way to explain grace is kindness that we don't deserve. If you look at it that way, it makes perfect sense that God isn't alone in His ability to give it out. In fact, it is His example we should look to when dealing with the people in our lives. That includes the ones we love and care about, as well as the ones we believe have harmed us or done us wrong.

In that sense, grace can have a sweet taste, yet in some cases, it can be a hard pill to swallow. It's easier to dole out grace to the ones we love but very difficult to administer to those we might identify as our enemies.

This is a truth to which I can fully relate.

Heavy Chains

When I was a kid, my dad let me down more times than I care to remember. Our mom always taught us to give him grace, to love and respect him no matter what. That wasn't terribly difficult for me to do. After all, he was my dad. I loved him, and I coveted a close relationship with him.

As a coach, I had a similar choice to make when Erick Barkley took a "leave of absence" from our St. John's team the night before the 2000 Big East Championship game. His decision had stemmed from a fight that took place in the locker room during the conference semifinal. I knew Erick's frustration was due to the unfair treatment he had received from the NCAA's yearlong investigation. The next afternoon, when he asked for the team to forgive him and let him come back, the decision to give him grace and allow him to return was an easy one to make. I cared deeply for all of my players and Erick was no exception.

What happened at the end of my tenure at St. John's, however, was a completely different story. While I shared some of the blame for a deteriorating relationship with the university's president, my firing after a rough 1-4 start during the 2003-04 season was completely unjustified. The truth of the matter was President Father Harrington was still upset over the fact that I had talked to Michael Jordan about the Wizards head coaching job and refused to discuss a contract extension with my agent Rob Ades.

To make things worse, accusations of how I lost control of the program (detailed in chapter one of this book) were trumped up after I was gone and used to help the media and the fans make sense of the senseless.

Make no mistake about it. I was angry. I was bitter. I felt betrayed. My reputation and character were under attack. But the thing that worried me the most was my wife's health. The pressure, the stress and the negative comments had impacted her physically and emotionally. Connie and I needed to get as far away from New York as possible, so we packed up and headed to Boca Raton, Florida.

Even after we moved and my wife started to feel better, we were still trying to find the strength to forgive. I didn't even want to think about forgiving the people or the institution that had done me wrong. It didn't just go away. I might not have dwelled on it or thought about it every day, but it was always there.

In 2005, about a year after moving to Florida and attending Spanish River Church, I accepted Christ as my Lord and Savior thanks to the evangelistic efforts of Pastor David Nicholas. As I spent more time in the Word through two weekly Bible studies, I started to catch a clearer glimpse of my problem. I was still full of unforgiveness and bitterness over what had happened at St. John's. I also began to realize how deeply hurt my wife still was. She was feeling the pain more than me. I had been busy working at ESPN. She was home alone and had more time to think about the past.

That's when I knew things needed to change. It was time for me to deal with the problem and become the spiritual leader in our home that God had called me to be. As I got to know His story better and better, I began to understand what forgiveness was supposed to look like. I also reflected on the many times I had needed to receive grace from others, those times when I had to cut or suspend a player from a team, or those times when I fell short in my responsibilities as a husband, father, friend, or coach.

But forgiveness is unnatural. In our humanity, it's much easier to hold on to bitterness than to show love, mercy and grace. That was something I could more clearly identify as I drew closer to Jesus and studied His teachings. It also allowed me to see the devil at work. Satan wants to see us angry, resentful and jealous. He wants to chain us up with those negative feelings and drag us down and keep us from moving forward. The longer we allow those chains to be placed on our lives, the heavier they become and the harder they are to remove.

Perhaps that's why moving past the situation at St. John's has been such a difficult battle. I've become stronger in the daily fight, but I must remain vigilant to not allow the enemy to take me back to that place.

Our departure from New York to Florida was unplanned and unexpected. However, in retrospect and without a doubt, it was a blessing of eternal consequence for my family. I believe God put us exactly where He wanted us to be. He placed us here and surrounded us with people that could disciple us on the real purpose of our lives. The community He selected for us was more interested in our eternal home than our past successes.

I hope I live long enough to where I can honestly say that I totally forgive anyone who has harmed me or anyone I think has wronged me. I don't know when I'll get there, but I know that Jesus Christ is already there, and I can only rest in His grace until that day comes.

The Good In The Bad

In the Old Testament, God used a young man named Joseph to illustrate the powerful message of divine grace. Joseph was Jacob's favorite son. His 11 brothers knew this to be true, especially after Jacob gave Joseph a beautiful coat (Genesis 37:3-4). Their growing jealousy turned to anger when Joseph told them about two vivid dreams. Both seemed to prophesy a time when they would all bow down to him (Genesis 37:5-11).

While tending their father's flocks, the brothers plotted to kill Joseph, but Reuben spoke up and convinced them to throw Joseph into a well instead. Reuben intended to save Joseph, but the other brothers had different plans. They sold him to some merchants who were passing through on their way to Egypt. The brothers tore Joseph's robe and covered it in animal blood to trick Jacob into thinking that his beloved son had been killed (Genesis 37:12-34).

In Egypt, one of Pharaoh's officials purchased Joseph from the merchants. Over the next several years he experienced God's favor amid some very challenging circumstances. When Joseph resisted the advances of his master's wife, he was put in prison after she falsely accused him of attacking her. While incarcerated, the warden put him in charge of the entire prisoner population (Genesis 39).

Joseph also became known for interpreting dreams. After two years in prison, he was called to appear before Pharaoh and explain to him a troubling vision of his own. God revealed to Joseph the meaning of the dream. Egypt was going to have seven years of plentiful harvest followed by seven years of famine. Pharaoh was amazed. He took heed of Joseph's interpretation and put the 30-year old Hebrew in charge of the entire nation (Genesis 41:1-41).

The amazing account of what happened next can be found in Genesis 42-45. During the famine, groups from the surrounding areas came to Egypt in desperate search for food. Jacob sent 10 of his remaining 11 sons to do the same. When Joseph heard they were in Egypt, he had them brought to him and accused them of being spies. The brothers did not recognize Joseph. He took the opportunity to test them. Joseph held Simeon captive and sent the others back with food. He commanded them to return with the missing brother, Benjamin, if they wanted Simeon to be freed.

When they returned, Joseph finally revealed his true identity. His brothers were very afraid. They knew Joseph would be justified in taking their lives. Instead, Joseph embraced his brothers and treated them like royalty. A few years later, after Jacob died, the brothers became fearful again. With their father gone, perhaps Joseph's forgiving spirit would fade. Nothing could have been further from the truth.

"You intended to harm me, but God intended it all for good. He brought me to this position so I could save the lives of many people." (Genesis 50:20/NLT)

Some might assume it was easy for Joseph to forgive his brothers because they were family, but what they did to him was very hurtful and caused him great physical and emotional pain. In the world's eyes, Joseph would have been well within his right to deny the help his brothers so desperately needed. Yet he was able to see the good things that came out of a bad situation. In the process, Joseph left behind a legacy of forgiveness and played an integral part in one of the greatest stories of grace ever told.

Everybody Needs Grace

When God sent Jesus to earth as a baby born to a virgin girl named Mary, it was the culmination of a plan that had been set into motion the moment Adam and Eve sinned in the Garden. God knew what needed to happen in order for mankind to be restored back to Him. Jesus would be required to live a sinless life and then die a harsh, cruel death on the Cross in order to shed His blood that would become a permanent and perfect offering for the sins of the world.

We didn't deserve it then, and there's nothing we can ever do to deserve it now or in the future. Jesus' supreme act of sacrifice will always be the greatest example of grace known to man. We are commanded to follow His example, but it takes a conscious effort. Giving grace and forgiving those who have done you wrong is a daily and often difficult choice. Here are five things that will help you do just that:

1. Set The Victim Free: If you hold on to bitterness and anger, it will create a sense of victimization and prevent you from growing into what God wants you to be. Don't let unforgiveness become an anchor that holds you down.

"Therefore, since we are surrounded by such a great cloud of witnesses, let us throw off everything that hinders and the sin that so easily entangles. And let us run with perseverance the race marked out for us." (Hebrews 12:1/NIV)

2. Let God Heal The Hurt: Many times it is our deep hurts that keep us from showing grace and forgiving others. Only God can mend a broken heart, but you have to allow Him inside so He can replace that hurt with His unconditional love.

"He heals the brokenhearted and binds up their wounds." (Psalm 147:3/NIV)

3. Embrace The Blessings: Everything is part of God's plan. Some things need to happen for you to get to where you need to be. Understanding this truth will help you turn the bad things into blessings. Being thankful for the journey will make it easier to root out bitterness and choose to forgive.

"And we know that in all things God works for the good of those who love him, who have been called according to his purpose." (Romans 8:28/NIV)

4. Forget The Past: In the movie *Unbroken*, Olympic athlete and World War II hero Louis Zamperini, portrayed by actor Jack O'Connell, made this powerful statement: "If you forgive, it's like it never happened. True forgiveness is complete and total."

When it comes to forgiveness, this is one of the hardest things to do. We tend to forget the good too quickly and remember the bad far too long. It might be impossible to completely forget past hurts, but we can choose not to think about them every minute of the day. And then God can bring new life to a dry and empty place.

"Forget the former things; do not dwell on the past. See, I am doing a new thing! Now it springs up; do you not perceive it? I am making a way in the wilderness and streams in the wasteland." (Isaiah 43:18-19/NIV)

5. Remember The Cross: Ultimately, there is no better encouragement to give grace than to look at the most powerful example ever displayed. When Jesus shed His precious blood and died for our sins, He showed us what it looks like to give something amazing to someone who has done nothing to deserve it. We can never live up to what Jesus did on the Cross, but we can remember His act of sacrifice every time we are contemplating whether or not to give grace to someone who has hurt us or done us wrong.

"For it is by grace you have been saved, through faith–and this is not from yourselves, it is the gift of God." (Ephesians 2:8/NIV)

When you give someone grace, what they do with it is of no consequence to you. It is entirely up to them. They can receive it graciously and turn from their hurtful ways or they can squander it and keep living the same. But when you forgive them, it allows you to get rid of anger, sadness, bitterness or hurts that have held you down like an anchor. Grace and forgiveness give you permission to move forward and fulfill the calling God has placed on your life.

Most importantly, it opens the doors of heaven so God can forgive you of *your* sins.

"For if you forgive other people when they sin against you, your heavenly Father will also forgive you. But if you do not forgive others their sins, your Father will not forgive your sins." (Matthew 6:14-15/NIV)

Everybody needs grace.

Study Questions

1. How do you define the word grace? Do you tend to give grace freely, or do you struggle with the concept of forgiveness and mercy?

2. Think about a time when it was easy for you to forgive someone. Now think about a time when it was difficult for you to forgive someone. What was different about those two situations? Were you able to resolve the difficult circumstance? Explain.

3. Can you relate to any of the stories referenced in this chapter (Coach Jarvis at St. John's, Joseph and his brothers, Jesus on the cross)? Explain.

4. Of the five keys to giving grace listed, which are generally comfortable for you to do? Which of those things presents a greater challenge? Is there one thing in particular that held you back more than the others? Explain.

5. Why do you think it can be so hard to give grace to someone who has hurt you? What human emotions and characteristics usually get in the way of grace and forgiveness?

6. Think about someone to whom you need to show grace today. What steps can you take that will help you forgive them and then move past the hurts that are holding you back?

Prayer

Lord, root out any bitterness, anger or pride in my heart that is keeping me from giving grace to those who have hurt me and wronged me. I need Your grace in my life so that I can show grace to others. I need Your healing for my heart so I can move forward and so You can complete the work You began in me. Help me to embrace the blessings, forget the past, and to never forget what You did on the Cross that made all of this possible. Amen.

AFTERWORD
Meet My Head Coach

He loved the thrill of the game, coaching a winning team, and the triumph of victory. Basketball was his life–until the winter it all came crashing down. During an unplanned time-out, Coach Mike Jarvis discovered what really matters and who makes life worth living. Read Mike's story of redemption–from an 11-year-old at a Celtics game to who he is today.

The Perfect Substitute

My love affair with basketball began on April 11, 1956, when my brother presented me with my very own basketball and a trip to see our favorite team, the Boston Celtics. Over the years I would refer to my eleventh birthday as one of the happiest days of my life–the others being the day I married my high school sweetheart, Connie, and the days my children, Michael and Dana, were born.

Thanks to my beloved brother Richard, Boston Celtics star player Bill Russell, and fiery coach Red Auerbach, my coaching career *unofficially* began that day in 1956. Since then, basketball has undergone many changes and evolved into one of the most popular team sports in the world. One thing has not changed: Championship teams usually have the best players and the best coaches.

In 1978, I officially began my head-coaching career at my alma mater, Cambridge Rindge and Latin High School in Cambridge, Massachusetts. During my first three years, we won three state championships, had the #1 team and #1 player in the state, and compiled an almost perfect record of 77–1. People often asked me how we lost that one game, and my answer was simple: "Patrick was sick." The Patrick I was referring to was Patrick Ewing, who went on to become an All-American and National Champion at Georgetown University, two-time Olympic gold medal winner, NBA All-Star with the New York Knicks, and a member of the Naismith Basketball Hall of Fame.

In 1985, I left Rindge and Latin and accepted the head coaching position for men's basketball at Boston University, followed by coaching stints at George Washington and St. John's. During those eighteen years, my teams appeared in fourteen post-season tournaments (nine NCAA's and five NIT's). We advanced to the Sweet Sixteen twice and came within three points of the Final Four in 1999, losing to Ohio State in the Elite Eight.

An Unplanned Time-Out, Courtesy of God

In the spring of 2003, I was on a roll. My coaching star was rising, and I thought life could only get better. My St. John's team had just won the NIT Championship in Madison Square Garden; I had an acting part in a motion picture movie, *The Perfect Score*, and I had co-authored my first book, *Skills for Life*. However, on December 19, after eighteen years and 360 victories as a Division I head coach, my life in basketball screeched to a sudden halt. I was fired–and my world came crashing down.

I was scared to death about my future. Not only was I out of work, but my reputation–and more importantly my character–were under attack. I didn't understand that this devastating situation was part of God's plan for me. In the process of remolding me for His purpose, He wanted my attention! God was letting me know that it wasn't about me, my family, or my career. Rather, it was all about Him and His story.

My wife and I agreed it was time to leave the Big Apple and start over in a new environment. Most people assumed we would move back to Cambridge or relocate to Maryland to be near our daughter and grandsons. My wife, however, had other plans. In May 2004, we moved into our new home in Boca Raton, Florida.

As we settled into our new life, we began looking for a church to attend and found Spanish River Church, right in our neighborhood. The first Sunday we visited, an older gentleman welcomed us at the front door. We found our seats and enjoyed the music and singing, followed by a message delivered by Pastor David Nicholas, the same man who had greeted us earlier! About halfway through his sermon, Connie and I looked at each other. We were in the right place. God had led us to our church home.

At the conclusion of the service, Pastor Nicholas made a special effort to speak with us. He told me he was a fan of mine, that he had played basketball at the University of Miami, and that he possessed a deadly hook shot. Two months later, Pastor David invited me to join his Friday morning Bible study with six other men from the church. I gladly accepted.

After a year of attending David's Bible study, I arrived on a Friday to discover that week's study had been cancelled. For some reason, I hadn't received the email, but David smiled and opened the door for me anyway. For the next hour and a half we engaged in a one-on-one conversation.

FIRST QUARTER: Playing by the Rules

After some small talk, David asked me something I will never forget: *If you died tonight, where would you wake up? Would you be in heaven with God, or would you be in hell with the devil?* It was a slam-dunk, or so I thought. Without any hesitation I told David I'd be with God in heaven. After all, I was a good person, attended church on a regular basis, and had never killed anybody. David laughed and told me he had a similar opinion of himself when he was young. He then explained that no matter how good I was, I could never measure up to God's standard of perfection.

David then shared some bad news with me. He told me how I had ignored God and consistently committed "crimes" against Him through my thoughts, words, and deeds. This made me a criminal in God's eyes. I had never thought of myself as a criminal and wasn't sure I agreed with his assessment, but I sat quietly and listened.

David then shared about Jesus and the Sermon on the Mount. He explained there is no such thing as a minor offense and that every sin is a big deal in God's eyes. David told me that God views unrighteous anger as a sin worthy of punishment, just as he views murder. I then realized my pastor must have seen me coach and observed anger as one of my many problems.

The clincher came when David recited the first commandment: *You must not have any other god but me* (Exodus 20:3). Now I *knew* he was talking about me, because for the first sixty years of my life I rarely put God first. I wasn't playing the game of life by God's rules, and I would have to be penalized for the "fouls" I had committed against Him.

SECOND QUARTER: On a Losing Team

David explained to me that because God is righteous and just, He couldn't accept me in my present condition. Like a referee, God had to hold me accountable for the actions and fouls I had committed against Him. David recited Romans 6:23: *For the wages of sin is death, but the free gift of God is eternal life through Christ Jesus, our Lord.* He explained that when we violate God's law, our punishment is death–spiritual, physical, and eternal separation from Him. David also made it perfectly clear that even if I only fouled (sinned) one time, it would be enough to get me ejected from the game.

HALF TIME

So how is it going for you? Are you winning or losing the game? If you're not where you'd like to be, remember this basic truth: The half-time score does not always reflect which team will win or lose the game. There's still another half to play–and anything can happen.

A good coach constantly reminds his players that the game is not over as long as time remains on the clock. Many coaches, myself included, often begin a halftime speech by delivering the *bad news*–everything that went wrong in the first half, followed by the *good news*–what went well. We emphasize that we can still win the game if we make the necessary adjustments, and we remind our players they cannot win the game by themselves.

God tells us the same thing in Ephesians 2:8-9: *God saved you by his grace when you believed. And you can't take credit for this; it is a gift from God. Salvation is not a reward for the good things we have done, so none of us can boast about it.* There is absolutely nothing we can do to make ourselves acceptable to God–no matter how talented we are, how hard we work, or how religious we try to be.

Basketball players are presented with various options at half time. They can continue to play the game in the same manner, give up, try to win on their own, or put their faith and trust in the head coach and play the game his way. This is the choice God presented to his first two players, Adam and Eve, and it's the same choice He presents to us today.

THIRD QUARTER: God's Perfect Substitute

Red Auerbach, former head coach of the Boston Celtics, revolutionized the game of basketball when he introduced the sixth man concept to the NBA. Unlike fellow coaches, Red would rest a star player and then put him in the action at just the right time, providing the team with the necessary lift to win the game. This extraordinary player would do for his teammates what they couldn't do for themselves, and ultimately drive them on to victory. During a ten-year-span that began in 1956, Red and his sixth man model won nine NBA Championships.

The good news is that God, the greatest head coach of all time, went one step further than Red. He sent the perfect substitute into the game of life for you and me. God the Father sent His Son, Jesus, to earth to become a man, so He could stand in and take the punishment for our sin.

The most quoted scripture of all time, John 3:16, says it all: *For God loved the world so much that he gave his one and only Son, so that everyone who believes in him will not perish but have eternal life.*

Jesus lived a perfect life, always doing what pleased His Father. At the age of 33, He was arrested, tried, convicted, and hung on a cross where He shed his precious blood for our sins. Many people have heard about the death of Christ, but they don't know why He died. After all, how could a man dying on a cross 2,000 years ago have anything to do with me today? The truth is, it has everything to do with me! God the Father, who knew all about me, took my sins and put them on Jesus *instead of on me.* When Jesus died, His body was placed in a tomb, and His enemies thought they had won the game. But on the third day, Jesus rose from the dead, overcoming sin and death. Through His death, He paid the penalty for all my sins. My sin debt was paid in full.

Jesus remained on earth for forty days and was seen by hundreds of people. Before He ascended into heaven, He told His followers to go into the world and tell everyone the *bad news* about their sin and the *good news* of what He had done through His death and resurrection. Those who believe both the bad news and the good news—and trust Jesus to save them from eternal condemnation—will have their sins forgiven and receive the free gift of eternal life.

David explained all of this to me the day of our cancelled Bible study. He shared that God wants everyone to hear, understand, and believe this amazing news. Unfortunately, though, not everyone will accept this truth. Those who reject God's grace and gift of salvation will remain lost forever.

FOURTH QUARTER: Time's Running Out

I returned home and went out back to sit in my favorite chair. I began reading a book David had written and sent home with me titled *Life: What's it all about?* The words came alive, and it felt like Jesus was right there talking to me. As I read, I thought about all the amazing people God had placed in my life and the incredible opportunities He had given me as a father, husband, teacher, and coach. I thought about losing my job at St. John's and how I felt like I'd lost it all, but now I realized it was actually the beginning of a much more meaningful life for me.

My mind drifted back over the years of my life. I recalled the sins I had committed against God with my thoughts, words and deeds— and how He never gave up on me. I thought about the time as a sophomore at Northeastern University when I quit the basketball team. I wondered where I would be today if Coach Dukeshire hadn't taken me back and later hired me as an assistant coach.

I continued to reflect. What would have happened if my wife, Connie, hadn't been able to get pregnant and give birth to our son, Michael? Would I have been drafted and shipped off to Vietnam with the rest of my buddies? Would I have returned home in a pine box or as a drug addict? What if Harvard hired me in 1977, and I hadn't had the opportunity to coach Patrick Ewing and the Cambridge Rindge and Latin Warriors? What if? *What if?*

FINAL TIME OUT

During the final timeout of a basketball game, I motivate my players to finish strong, give it their all, and never give up. Hall of Fame basketball coach John Wooden of UCLA once said, "Don't let what you can't do interfere with what you can. You can't save yourself but you can trust the one who can."

It was with this realization that I turned to the next page of David's book and read a suggested prayer of salvation. I made this prayer my own.

Lord Jesus, I want you to become my Head Coach. I come to you, acknowledging that I am a sinner and cannot make myself acceptable to You through my own efforts. I believe You went to the Cross as my substitute, to be judged in my place, and by doing so You saved me from the judgment I deserve. You did for me what I could not do for myself. I trust You to give me a new life that works, and I know You are the only One who can give it to me. Furthermore, I believe with all of my heart and soul that You are the way, the truth, and the life, and that no one can come to the Father except through You. Lord Jesus, please give me the necessary strength and wisdom to live like You so that I may successfully complete the work You sent me here to do. Amen.

I then closed the deal by signing the contract in black and white. I pray that you will do the same.

I, Michael D. Jarvis, trusted in Jesus Christ as my Lord and Savior on April 29, 2005, and therefore I now belong to God forever, because the Lord has forgiven my sins and given me the gift of eternal life.

POST GAME

The next evening, Connie and I met David and his wife for dinner. David immediately knew by the look on my face that something special had happened. I told him I had accepted Jesus Christ as the Lord of my life. I shared that I finally knew why Connie and I had moved to Boca Raton, and it wasn't for the sunshine. God had led us to a place where I would come to know Christ through hearing and understanding the bad news about myself and the good news of Jesus Christ.

Three years later, with the help of Pastor Nicholas, my next door neighbor Milt Keslow, my long time friend Peter Kramer, the men in my Bible study group, and countless members of the Boca Raton community, God allowed me to return to the coaching profession as the head basketball coach for Florida Atlantic University. In January 2011, I attended David's funeral at Spanish River Church and stood with more than 300 people David had personally recruited to play on the Lord's team.

As a new believer in Christ, my life has taken on a whole new meaning! I've given priority to reading and studying God's playbook, the Bible, on a daily basis. David once told me that if I read the Bible for fifteen minutes a day, I could read the Old and New Testaments in one year. Recently I completed it for the fourth time, and each time I've gained a better understanding of how much God loves me and how He wants me to think, speak, and act. My wife and I host a Bible study every Wednesday in our home. I have also been able to grow in my faith by listening to a local Christian radio station, Moody Radio, 89.3 FM.

So faith comes from hearing, that is, hearing the Good News about Christ (Romans 10:17).

Jesus said that those who receive God's gift of life will demonstrate it through their lives. Today I'm a better person than I used to be, but I still have a long way to go. On occasion, I allow my pride and sinful nature to rear its ugly head. The biggest difference now is that I immediately know when I have offended God, and I know that I am not alone, because I have the Holy Spirit living within me.

Before I became a believer in Christ, basketball was my idol, my god. It had an adverse effect on many aspects of my life, including my relationship with my wife. Now, however, I understand God wants me to love Him with all of my heart, soul, and mind. *Nothing* is to take the place of my relationship with Him.

Today, with Christ as my focus, the other areas of my life fall into their rightful place. I pray each day that God will give me the strength to be patient, loving, and humble, and to have the ability to forgive. I know that as I imitate Christ, my life will be enhanced, as will be the lives of those around me.

Furthermore, as a born again Christian, God has saved me from an eternal life in hell and has commissioned me to share the Good News of Jesus Christ. In closing, I would like to ask you the same question David asked me: *If you were to die tonight, where would wake up?*

The perfect substitute, Jesus Christ, is waiting to get into the game for you—just as He did for me.

With Much Love,

Coach Mike Jarvis

*All scripture quoted from the New Living Translation.

INDEX

ENDORSEMENTS

"Mike Jarvis is one of my very special friends. I am a lucky guy because he takes friendship to the highest level. I am so pleased that he has taken some time to write this fabulous book. In the book he gives his readers an opportunity to see firsthand the magic he has shown in developing players and teams in extraordinary fashion. This will be a great read not only for coaches and athletes, but also for the business world and for parents. I especially believe parents will benefit from reading this book as much as I benefited from being Mike's friend." – Mike Krzyzewski, Five-Time NCAA Championship Men's Basketball Coach, Duke University

"As you read this book, I hope that Coach Jarvis' experiences inspire you to find your purpose in life. I also hope that his story challenges you to find someone that you can mentor and influence just like he did for me in my life." – Patrick Ewing, Hall of Fame NBA Center and Two-Time Olympic Gold Medalist

"Everybody Needs A Head Coach is a refreshingly transparent look into Mike Jarvis' highly successful coaching career. Coach Jarvis shares both his victories and his defeats in a way that ultimately points readers to the transformative biblical teachings of Jesus. This is a fantastic read for any coaches, athletes, parents or business leaders looking to gain a better understanding of their greater purpose in life." – Pat Williams, Co-Founder and Senior Vice President, Orlando Magic, and Author of 21 Great Leaders

"When is the best time to plant an oak tree? Twenty years ago. When is the next best time? Today. If you are over twenty and you are something less than a hot, on fire, going for it, no holds barred, Jesus loving believer, then today is your day. Twenty-three biblical principles coupled with Coach Mike Jarvis' expert story telling is a winning combination. Take them to heart and you'll have victory in Jesus." – Jay Carty, Founder, Yes! Ministries, and Co-Author of *Coach Wooden: One-On-One* and *Coach Wooden's Pyramid of Success*

"I first met Mike Jarvis in the 1970's, when he was the legendary coach at Cambridge Rindge and Latin, guiding Patrick Ewing both on and off the court. He's still the go-to guy when you want to know about life or how to get to the Elite Eight." – Hall of Fame Sportscaster Lesley Visser

"I can't explain how much Coach Jarvis means to me. He was my coach at the 1981 McDonalds East/West Game 1981 in Wichita, Kansas. The one thing I remember that week was that he gave me the assignment to be the starting point guard on our roster. He gave me confidence and leadership tools because of his belief in my ability. Coach Jarvis is without a doubt a man of high integrity and character." – Buzz Peterson, NBA scout, Charlotte Hornets, and former NCAA head basketball coach

"Mike and I worked together at Northeastern University many years ago. In reading this book, I can see that he hasn't lost his edge or his purpose. *Everybody Needs A Head Coach* is a very insightful look into his career and his strong motivation and focus. It gives a nice glimpse at how he achieved great success and how he dealt with adversity. Mike should be congratulated for this effort. Readers should take a look at what he has to say." – Jim Calhoun, Hall of Fame and Three-Time NCAA Championship Men's Basketball Coach, University of Connecticut

"Mike Jarvis is an outstanding basketball coach and has been a terrific teacher of the game and a visionary leader for decades. He has not only been a teacher and a coach, but he has been a lifelong learner as well, and the lessons he shares in *Everybody Needs A Head Coach* are invaluable for any parent, teacher, coach or player." – Jay Bilas, College Basketball Analyst, ESPN

"We need men such as Mike Jarvis to be role models and coaches for young men today, and his book articulates why. There is a thirst in this land for men of faith and courage to make a stand and reclaim this nation's honor and heritage. That can only be done by way of a recommitment to our Judeo-Christian faith principles, which Coach Jarvis presents in his timely book. With men like Coach Mike Jarvis leading the way, we will restore this Republic and servant-based Christian manhood." – Lieutenant Colonel Allen West, Retired, Bronze Star recipient and former U.S. Congressman

"The word 'coach' was first used in the 1500s in England. A coach was a horse-drawn carriage used to transport a person of importance from where he or she wanted to be, could be, needed to be, or ought to be going. That is what Mike Jarvis did his best to do with all of his players. Coach Jarvis' new book *Everybody Needs A Head Coach* is loaded with wisdom and uplifting stories. He is a true gentleman and the kind of man that is the epitome of a real coach!" – Dale Brown, Head Men's Basketball Coach, LSU, 1972-1997, College Basketball Hall of Fame inductee

"*Everybody Needs A Head Coach* is a must read for every young coach in the country. In fact, every individual can benefit from the lessons described in this book. Coach Jarvis takes a very sincere look within and encourages others to learn from his mistakes. Very impressive–and very real!" – Lon Kruger, Head Men's Basketball Coach, University of Oklahoma

"Mike Jarvis has authored a book that reminds us that life is a journey not a destination and that God has positioned Himself to be our head coach throughout. *Everybody Needs A Head Coach* shows us that we are playing the game of life with a loving, compassionate, gracious, merciful, good, and powerful God that has committed Himself to teach us, encourage us, and fill us with His strength and wisdom throughout our life's journey." – Jim Haney, Executive Director, National Association of Basketball Coaches

"Mike Jarvis has combined the power of storytelling and personal experience and faith, with the word of God to write an inspiring and instructive book. It's a practical, principled guide on the impact of effective coaching, and the transformative power of being effectively coached by the ultimate Head Coach, Jesus Christ." – Clark Kellogg, VP of Player Relations and former NBA player, Indiana Pacers, and lead college basketball analyst, CBS Sports

"To know Mike Jarvis is quite special. To have had an opportunity to work with him is to have been in the company of a superior person. You will feel the touch of Jarvis as you benefit from the reading of *Everybody Needs A Head Coach*. – Tom "Satch" Sanders, Former Harvard University Men's Basketball Coach, and Eight-Time NBA Champion and Basketball Hall of Fame inductee, Boston Celtics

"Coach Jarvis and I came to the Lord late in our coaching careers. It is never too late for any of us to make the most important commitment of our lives. It is nice to know that Coach is now my brother in Christ." – Daniel Miles, Head Men's Basketball Coach, Oregon Institute of Technology

"Every coach and parent interested in getting the next generation to listen should begin with this book. While reading, I found myself in one of the most powerful conversations I have ever had. Coach Jarvis spoke with a fatherly tone and what felt like a concerned hand on my back. We began a journey together, to help me reach my potential...as a son, husband, father, and mostly a Christian leader. Coach Jarvis, thank you for the invitation into your life and the challenge of beginning mine." – Sean Hanrahan, Head Men's Basketball Coach, Warner University

"This book will take you on a journey of inspiration and leave you yearning for more by providing a fresh take on discovering God's purpose and 'story' for each of our lives, while showing how transformative a coach can be when you live your life as a master teacher." – Dr. Manny Ohonme, Founder, President and CEO, Samaritan's Feet International, and author of the best-selling book Sole Purpose.

"Real transformation makes us want to know the source of that change. Watching Coach Mike Jarvis find true purpose has been an encouragement to many and has helped move others towards Jesus, the source of transformation. Coach Jarvis teaches principles that will help anyone to find purpose. *Everybody Needs A Head Coach* is easy to read, easy to apply, and can be a valuable resource to use with others." – Eric Nelson, Director of Global Sports/Basketball, Athletes in Action

"*Everybody Needs A Head Coach* is a must read. Whether you are a coach, an athlete, a lawyer, a schoolteacher, or a banker, this book is full of life lessons that can help us all. Coach Jarvis reminds us about the importance of Christ-centered living, and that, regardless of our positions in life, we all need a mentor and a Head Coach to help us achieve our purpose." – Tommy McClelland, Director of Athletics, Louisiana Tech University

"Mike has put together a great teaching book for parents, coaches, mentors, teens and children. There are lessons for all of us from "everybody has a story" to "getting rid of pride," to "living with humility" and "everyone needs a second chance." All from a wonderful teacher-coach and an even better friend." – George Blaney, Former Head Men's Basketball Coach, Holy Cross and Seton Hall, and Former President, National Association of Basketball Coaches

"All of us at times need to take an inventory of ourselves and find meaning in life's ups and downs. Regardless of one's religious beliefs, *Everybody Needs A Head Coach* provides a valuable lesson and practical study guide about how we may find a path to self-improvement, perseverance through adversity, and true purpose in life. Mike Jarvis is masterful in providing insight through the lens of real world experience how one can embark on a path of living a more fulfilling life for themselves and others. Truly a great read!" – Dr. Robert A. Chernak, Senior Vice Provost and Senior Vice President Emeritus, The George Washington University, Washington, DC

"I love being inspired and this book does that! Coaches need to help players with the development of skills, help them learn to work together, to win and to lose and to become a family. In his wonderful book, Mike Jarvis also eloquently brings in the spiritual aspect. Everyone needs to read this book. Your mind will be enriched and your heart lifted." – Jim Burson, Solution-Based Basketball®, author of The Golden Whistle and The Daily Nugget

"Coach Jarvis has taken his life story and broken it into individual segments that give meaning to life on an everyday basis. His ability to motivate basketball players is well documented. This book takes it another step. It can motivate anyone regardless of class, race, etc. It's tremendous how his life stories are paralleled to biblical characters, and most importantly, Jesus Christ. The probing questions at the end of each chapter will make each reader evaluate their own life and hopefully, make them a better individual. I endorse what Coach has done. Well done good and faithful servant." – Don Lane, Retired Basketball Coach, Transylvania University, and member of Kentucky Athletic Hall of Fame

"Mike Jarvis will forever be "Coach" to me. He is my friend, role model, teacher, leader and a true inspiration in my life. Coach Jarvis' story and testimony are vivid lessons of what God can do in a person's life when we release ourselves from our own prideful ways and allow God to work miracles. *Everybody Needs A Head Coach* is inspirational and touching. Coach Jarvis' personal testimony is an awesome lesson of the healing and restorative power of God!" – Kevin Henderson, Chief Executive Officer, the College Basketball Experience and NCAA Basketball Hall of Fame

"This is a must read not only for coaches but also for those in business as well as student athletes. With many coaches fearful of sharing their faith across America today, it's refreshing to see that Coach Jarvis has found his faith in Christ and is not ashamed. *Everybody Needs A Head Coach* brings truthfulness and insight to a sport and profession that we all have witnessed can get away from the character and integrity that we all need in this business." – Tony Pierce, Assistant Football Coach, Savannah State University

"*Everybody Needs A Head Coach* is both inspirational and entertaining and should be in every coach's library. It is the answer to the question, 'Why do I coach?' and helps the coach understand how he should coach. I believe God will use this book to put Coach Jarvis in the Final Four. A true championship coach has been taught by his head coach, 'The Master Coach.'" – Dale Clayton, Vice President of Coaches Ministry, Nations of Coaches

"Mike Jarvis is a very special person. Together we authored *Skills For Life: The Fundamentals You Need To Succeed* and have presented the material to thousands of students and adults. Mike's new book venture is not only heartwarmingly honest and straight forward but is a must read for anybody who seeks greater peace, more direction and is a superb guide for life and the world we live in." – Jonathan B. Peck, Co-Author, *Skills For Life*

"Everyone has a story! Mike drives home this powerful truth in *Everybody Needs A Head Coach*. In a masterful way, Coach Jarvis connects his story to our stories weaving in powerful principles and timeless truth in such a way that it ultimately connects us to God's bigger story. I love Mike and I love the way his life, honesty, wisdom, and heart for helping people penetrate these pages." – Tommy Kiedis, Senior Pastor, Spanish River Church, Boca Raton, Fla.

"Mike has combined the best of both worlds in his new book. His ability to tie lessons with life is spot on. The lessons are great reminders for all of us and the stories show us how we may be able to incorporate those lessons into our own lives. No question, it's a book worth reading with ideas worth applying." – Kevin Eastman, Vice President for Basketball Operations, Los Angeles Clippers

"Coach Mike Jarvis has provided critical insights into the development of a new generation of leaders. He has demonstrated the vital relationship between the vocation of coaching and God's divine guidance. To do this, Mike offers biblical insights to a variety of life issues and dilemmas. Anyone who is serious about leading young people to excellence in their endeavors, and more importantly, Christian commitment and service should read and apply these principles. I strongly recommend this book be used as a text for church, educational and service groups." – William Phillips DeVeaux, Presiding Prelate, Second Episcopal District, African Methodist Episcopal Church

"Coach Mike Jarvis is a friend, mentor, role model, and a fellow Northeastern University Alumni. I am honored to be able to talk about Coach Jarvis the man, husband, father, grandfather, coach, teacher, and friend, but more importantly God's spokesperson in the field of athletics. I am so happy that he has taken the time to write this amazing book, because we all sometimes lose sight of the fact that whatever we do, we are still just servants for the Lord. I thank Coach Jarvis for reminding us of that in *Everybody Needs A Head Coach*." – Eugene Marshall Jr., Director of Athletics, Hampton University

"*Everybody Needs A Head Coach* is a great read filled with up close and personal inside stories of many basketball greats. It is the story of a journey, the journey of a man to succeed as head coach in the rough, tough world of basketball. On several occasions, it seemed as though he had reached his goal but then the pieces would start to fall apart. One night he discovered that he was not the head coach, but that there was a Head Coach to whom he was answerable. Mike Jarvis humbled himself before that ultimate Head Coach and everything changed because Mike's heart was changed." – Nori Nicholas, The Church Planting Network

"*Everybody Needs A Head Coach* is a compelling must-read book that takes you into the world of one of the greatest college coaches in the history of basketball. Mike Jarvis is a skilled coach and is also a gifted screenwriter (*Court of Kings*, about his years in basketball at Cambridge Rindge and Latin). He has done a superb job of bringing his experiences to the reader. This is a fascinating story that everyone will enjoy." – Richard Warren Rappaport, Esq., The Law Firm, Richard Warren Rappaport, Esq., Boca Raton, Florida

"*Everybody Needs A Head Coach* is one of the most unique and inspiring books I've ever had the pleasure to read. Throughout the book we learn lessons that can only be given by a man who has been to both the mountaintops and the valleys of life. This book is seasoned by the struggles, disappointments and triumphs that only come from a lifetime of experience. Reading and applying the lessons of this book will make you a better person and most importantly a better Christian. At its conclusion, you will appreciate the transparency and wisdom of this wonderful man. Thank you Mike for sharing your story and His." – Rev. Jonathan Vazquez, Senior Pastor, Bethlehem Church of Potts Camp, MS and Bethlehem Church of Starkville, MS; Superintendent, Mississippi District of the Assemblies of the Lord Jesus Christ

"Coach Jarvis has had a profound influence on me over the course of my career. I have watched and learned as he has coached and mentored young people by the hundreds and helped to unleash their full potential while ushering them toward adulthood. His impression on the Greater Boston area is indelible. I can only imagine that as he has moved throughout the nation, his positive sphere of influence and impact has simply widened." – J. Keith Motley, Chancellor, University of Massachusetts Boston

"Mike has revealed the true core of coaching. His experiences expose the importance of personal relationships, trust development, and the ability to inspire others while leading a team. His story is relevant for anybody seeking guidance in becoming a successful servant leader in today's world." – Ben Braun, Former Pac-10 Coach of the Year at Cal with 615 career wins and current college TV analyst

"I played one full season for Coach Jarvis at Northeastern University. That year was the most gratifying year in all of my athletic life. Coach Jarvis was very instrumental in preparing me for what was to come. In *Everybody Needs A Head Coach,* Coach Jarvis shares his personal experiences in life. His stories relate to all people. His stories are aligned with biblical principles. I am most impressed with how Coach Jarvis and his co-author Chad Bonham give the glory to God. Their message has given me a great sense of inspiration." – Sifu William J. Rosary Jr., Grandmaster of Yang Style Tai Chi Chuan

"There's only one Head Coach in life that will meet all your needs and help you fulfill your God-given purpose. Mike Jarvis introduces you to that Head Coach in his book." – Bill Hobbs, President and Founder, Urban Youth Impact

"Coach Jarvis' book is past due for many players, coaches, athletic directors, and team owners and executives. I am trusting the Lord that this will a great harvesting tool for the Kingdom of God." – Rev. Ike Pritchett, Edifying Ministries, Richmond, Virginia

For speaking and signed books:

Coach Mike Jarvis
8121 Desmond Drive
Boynton Beach, FL 33472
561-877-4646
coachmikejarvis.com
coachmikejarvis@gmail.com